The Call to Prayer

Intimate Moments with God

Forrest Hemphill Yanke, D. Phil., LCSW, LMFT

En Route Books and Media, LLC

Saint Louis, MO

Visit https://www.forrestyankebooks.com/

Make the time

En Route Books and Media, LLC
5705 Rhodes Avenue
St. Louis, MO 63109

Cover image: Photograph by Kenneth Hoeck

Copyright © 2022 Forrest Hemphill Yanke

ISBN-13: 978-1-956715-44-6
Library of Congress Control Number: 2022936107

Table of Contents

Testimonials

"Forrest has written a beautiful invitation to deepen our prayer through reflection on her own personal prayer journey. Wherever you may be in your own prayer journey, just beginning or more experienced, you will find something to enrich your prayer life through the pages of this book."

Msgr. Keith Brennan
Pastor, Our Lady Star of the Sea
Ponte Vedra Beach, Florida

"This book offers helpful theological information, resources, and encouragement for both those who desire to begin a new prayer life, and for those who feel called to deepen an already established prayer routine."

Adrienne Novotny, M.Ed.
Acting Director
The Cenacle
Our Lady of Divine Providence House of Prayer
Clearwater, Florida

"After many years of experimentation and experience, Forrest Yanke presents a recipe for prayer, using as a foundation her charismatic Carmelite spirituality, while blending in portions of Ignatian reflection, and the rich nutrition of Eucharistic and Marian devotion. Good food for thought!"

Sister Mary Margaret, O.P.
Prioress
Monastery of the Infant Jesus
Cloistered Contemplative Dominican Nuns
Lufkin, TX

Dedication

This book is dedicated to Mother Mary, Our Lady of Perpetual Help and St. Joseph, my spiritual companions along the way, and in memory of brother Robert, a soulmate, who loved the spiritual life and was a beautiful, creative writer.

Special Acknowledgment

Special acknowledgment concerning the front cover art: Kenneth Hoeck, who provided the artwork for the cover, is a Licensed Mental Health Counselor, with a trauma focus; and resides in Ponte Vedra Beach, Florida. He states that he has been fascinated with healing from an early age. "The image presented is developed from my practice of contemplative reception of images. It is a blend of three of the images that came to me in prayer. The living waters flowing down in Yosemite, the birds speak of the Holy Spirit's wildness and freedom, and the St. Augustine statue is a poignant image with hands to Heaven and earth, humans being conduits and temples of all of this." Kenneth is a practicing Catholic, "happily" married to Grace for almost thirty-two years, and has two "dear" sons, William and Matthew.

Foreword

We are all spiritual beings. Not like angels, who are pure spirit, but like all humans, creations with a body and a soul.

We do much to care for the body. The spiritual dimension sometimes/many times is overlooked, forgotten, and relegated to the dim background of life. If that happens, there will always be an unfulfilled heart. We either know God and love and serve Him. Or we don't know God and are always on a quest to find Him, however dim the understanding might be.

But the fact is, we all—without exception—need to tend to the spiritual dimension of life. The first and foremost element of spirituality is faith, a foundational belief in God that brings us into relationship with our Creator. It is here that we discover our own true and deepest identity. Blessed are all who know their God and Creator; they know themselves.

A person without a spiritual grounding in life will always be searching and never satisfied or fulfilled. Spiritual grounding brings balance and equilibrium to all aspects of life. It completes us. Jesus taught us to pray always. It was not an idle suggestion.

The spiritual life breathes in prayer. As fish need water and as we all need oxygen, the human spirit needs prayer. Daily, well-balanced, consistent prayer is lifeblood to the spiritual life.

In this book *The Call to Prayer: Intimate Moments with God*, we find a valuable resource for the prayer life. It's not an academic treatise on prayer, but a valuable witness from someone who prays and has learned to pray over the years. This "someone" is not a nun, theologian, priest, or monk, but a laywoman with authentic personal experience of faithful prayer life. And this puts her in a unique position to inspire many.

The church tradition has a storehouse of experience and time-tested methods of prayer, dimensions of prayer, forms of prayer, and ways of praying. Saints have taught much about prayer. There are devotions that are time honored. There are dimensions in prayer waiting to be explored.

Here is a personal witness of one woman's journey of faith and her growth as a praying person, discovering spiritual treasures along the way.

Forrest Yanke's book is encouraging to read and stimulates a desire to learn and experience the riches being offered to us all: humble laity, educated theologians, seekers after God.

We are all on the journey of faith and can benefit from the wisdom of those who also walk the road of prayer.

Fr. Richard McAlear, OMI
Ministry of Hope & Healing
www.frmac.org
Fr. Richard McAlear is an internationally renowned

speaker and retreat director who has brought the healing power of Jesus Christ to countless audiences and individuals. He has authored numerous books, and his teachings about healing, prayer and deliverance are captured in audio and video titles. "Fr. Mac," as he's affectionately known, is a long-time member of the Association of Christian Therapists, served as a vocation director in Washington, DC, and was on staff at Ave Maria University. He now devotes himself full time to the nonprofit "Ministry of Hope & Healing."

Author's Note

Have you ever had a longing in your heart that wouldn't go away?

Jesus entered the temple area and drove out all those engaged in selling and buying there. He overturned the tables of the money changers and the seats of those who were selling doves. And he said to them, 'It is written: 'My house shall be a house of prayer, but you are making it a den of thieves.' (Matthew 21: 12-14)

For a number of years, living in Panama City, Florida, I longed for a house of prayer for all peoples. There was such need. In fact, the need was abundant. I loved praying with people – in my clinical practice – in my prayer group – or wherever the opportunity existed; and the need was there. In fact, the need was abundant!

So, I envisioned an actual structure or house, where people in pain or struggling could come all hours of the day and receive prayer, unconditional love, healing in body, mind, or spirit, and just "be" in the Lord's presence.

The call from the Lord was so strong in my heart that I finally "worked up" the courage to ask for, and receive, an appointment with the bishop at the time. The bishop said yes to a house of prayer and referred me to the vicar general of the diocese for discussion of the matter.

I made this appointment also, and kept it, eager to share my vision. But the house of prayer was not to be. The persecution directed at me was intense. Coupled with the fact that we were about to move to another part of Florida, the house of prayer that I dreamed about was not built. However, the dream did not leave me. And a different kind of house, without a structure, was later built......

It had become clearer to me that my first understanding and experience with a house of prayer was at Our Lady of Divine Providence House of Prayer in Clearwater, Florida. What an influence Diane Brown and Barbara Shlemon, foundresses of the House with Adrian and Ron Novotny, all ACT (Association of Christian Therapists and now AC-THeals) members at the time.

In those small beginnings: a small house and people from their prayer groups, there was prayer, holiness, and healing in body, mind, and spirit. I learned that Jesus wants prayer, wants to heal through prayer, and wants it for all people. I was, of course, prayed for and received much healing, particularly in the spiritual area, for which I am grateful. These early experiences affected me deeply and became part of the "cornerstone" of all that I am called to be.

Still wondering about that house of prayer dream within me..... I attended an Intercessors of the Lamb Conference in

Omaha, Nebraska, that July 4th week in the summer. This turned out to be a particular kind of spiritual liberation that was life-changing!

When I asked for a house of prayer, and was prayed with by two very holy sisters, a different Word than what I hoped for, or expected from the Lord, was given to me. I was so surprised when Sister Rita said to me emphatically: "You are to become a house of prayer." "What - I thought...I already pray night and day. What could this possibly mean?"

Years later, I realize now that Jesus had a distinct "building project" for me. My building was the "growing" of that structure "within" rather than "without." It had no walls. With the fruit of much individual prayer, I began to read more about prayer, teach classes on prayer, practice healing prayer for others when called upon, and co-facilitate a prayer group. I became a spiritual director guiding others in their prayer journeys. Jesus was building that house of prayer within me, and I was immersed and content.

This book is written with the sincere hope and prayer that you will open yourself to the call to intimacy, through prayer, that God desires to have with you. Will you allow him to "build a house of prayer in you?" Scripture tells us that he has called you by name, and that you are his. And, further, that you are held in the palm of his hand; that he knew you before you were born.

God has already connected with us, and we have a choice of how, when, and to what depth we will connect with him.

And what a gift—touches of his presence—that can permeate each moment of our daily lives.

In my faith journey, building my house of prayer, I find that there is nothing more fulfilling than those "touches" from God, where you "know that you know" he is with you: living with you, loving you, forgiving you, and calling you to be his precious child. You want to stay in those moments. And if you say yes and linger, it is God's greatest fulfillment. As Jesus said on the cross: "I thirst." You can satisfy his thirst.

As you read this book, I invite you to bow your head, so together we can ask the Father of all mercies to send his Holy Spirit to refresh you, enlighten you, and guide you. And to build his house of prayer within you. And please know that I have sought God to touch you, heal you, and encourage you through his son, Jesus Christ—the Lamb of God, the Bread of Life, the Good Shepherd—to a fresh and more profound life of prayer.

Come Holy Spirit and enkindle in us the fire of your love! And may our Mother Mary, St. Joseph, and my favorite Carmelite saints: Teresa of Jesus (Avila), Therese of the Child Jesus and the Holy Face (Lisieux), and John of the Cross, accompany you in prayer to those innermost places within your soul where God desires to reveal himself to you.

I ask this in the Holy Name of Jesus, Amen.

CHAPTER 1

Toward Intimacy with God:
Beginnings of Prayer

What do you pray about? How do you know when to pray? *What is prayer, anyway?*

Have you ever asked yourself, and reflected upon, these three very important questions? I truly had not considered the topic until well into adulthood.

Growing up as a Christian, the custom in our home and in our church was to turn to God in prayer, in the rituals of grace before meals and bedtime prayers. Like many others have experienced, prayer was something I did without much thought about why or with a sense of relationship. In my home, we didn't talk about prayer.

I witnessed my father kneeling every morning at his bedside and praying, but I did not know what he prayed; and I never thought to ask him. God was all around, but the idea of talking to him in conversation like I do now, a kind of ongoing dialogue, was foreign to me.

I had never truly reflected upon a deeper meaning of prayer until some years ago when I moved to Florida. Then, astonishingly, these questions about prayer launched a new journey of faith.

1

This book is about that prayer journey, which I am still enjoying. I'm truly passionate about prayer—doing it, talking about it, reading about it, and teaching it. And that's the reason for this book.

In my mind, prayer as a process can be likened to a beautiful stream that flows gently at times, rushes over rocks at times, may be full of beautiful fish here or there, but is always moving, dynamic, changing—and yet, somehow the same.

So here is how that journey to prayer began anew.

Shortly after I relocated to Florida, I noticed through an advertisement in a local newspaper that a Transactional Analysis training group met monthly in a local Christian psychotherapy practice, The Cornerstone. I was curious, wanting to join the group, and I approached the person who coordinated it.

I was of the Presbyterian denomination. I did not blend my faith into my clinical work but was interested in the psychological training and didn't feel that the denomination mattered. Little did I know that the Lord would bring me to a "spiritual awakening" as a result of participating in what I thought was *only* a psychological training group.

It started when I asked the person in charge a simple question: "What is the monthly fee?" I hardly expected the response: "I'll have to pray about it."

Well, this answer was so strange to me; I didn't know what to think. Here was a business transaction, and it called for *prayer*? I asked myself two questions: "Does this matter need prayer?" (The "why") and "What would there be to pray about?" (The "what").

At that time, I believed that praying to God was to be about more serious things—crises in the world, personal calamities, sicknesses, difficulties with relationships, etc. I imagined I was bothering God with these kinds of questions, like, "God, will you find me a parking spot?" (That seemed like a trivial question back then; however, I ask that question now!)

† † †

In Luke 1:18, we read: "And he told them a parable, to the effect that they ought always to pray and not lose heart."

St. Teresa of Jesus (Avila), foundress of the Discalced Carmelite Order, and a master on contemplative prayer, said: "...mental prayer is nothing else, in my opinion, but being on terms of friendship with God, frequently conversing in secret with Him Who, we know, loves us."[1]

Fr. Jacques Philippe in *Thirsting for Prayer* writes:

To pray is to spend time freely with God just for the joy of being together. It is to love, because giving our time means giving our lives. Love does not mean primarily to do something for the other person, it means being there with them. Prayer trains us to be there with God, in a simple act of loving attention.[2]

What a new way of thinking: that prayer was a personal relationship and helps us recognize we are loved. It was a breath of fresh air! Because my heavenly Father loves me, that means I can ask him for help, even in the smallest matters? And I don't have to wait for the big ones? I finally understood that group leader's response: "I'll have to pray about it."

† † †

In a second grade Presbyterian Sunday School class, I recall embroidering a very simple red cloth bookmark that read "God is love." And yet, did I really know him as love? I remember *feeling* the love of my Sunday School teacher and kept a picture of her in one of my scrapbooks, but I did not associate that as the love of God. I think I knew God *intellectually* only.

I didn't "get" that God showed his love through others as I know now that he does through the Sacraments of the Eucharist and Reconciliation. He had to connect to me *in love* through my prayer life.

As a child, I didn't know how to experience a personal relationship with God. My family was involved in the church, and I did the usual church activities: Attending church and Sunday School on Sundays, singing in the choir, Vacation Bible School, summer camp, and youth group. But these activities were related to the "doing" with God.

In pondering prayer, a scripture comes to mind, 1 Thessalonians 5:16-18:

Rejoice always. Pray without ceasing. In all circumstances give thanks, for this is the will of God for you in Christ Jesus.

Max Lucado in his book, *Before Amen: The Power of a Simple Prayer,* writes:

Prayer is not a privilege for the pious, nor the art of a chosen few. Prayer is simply a heartfelt conversation between God and his child. My friend he wants to talk with you. Even now, as you read this book, he taps at the door.[3]

Once I was involved with the training group, I noticed the participants prayed before decisions, after decisions, and often in-between, and it was a way of life in their personal as well as professional journeys. I began to see that when you love someone, you talk to them often, and they loved talking to God all the time; and this was new for me.

The training group acknowledged a holistic approach to

treatment that held fast to the spiritual dimension: a dimension not taught traditionally in the psychotherapy field. I came to understand, however, that dealing with one's spiritual views and relationship to God was essential in guiding one into better mental and physical health.

Psychology, by itself, I discovered, could be considered limited in offering an approach to wholeness and health, as it did not include the fullness of God's life in the person. For instance, discerning God's will for the person brought the truth of his/her existence rather than a limited and self-centered view of oneself.

Suddenly, only praying personally at meals and at bedtime didn't work any longer for me. I found God wanted more, and I learned to pray before, during, and after client visits. That's what led me to answer to the third question I proposed at the beginning of this chapter: "What is prayer?" And the Holy Spirit led me to the answers of the "why" and "what" of prayer as well.

Who *was* the Holy Spirit? I needed to better understand this third person of the Trinity. Through the influence and invitation of members of the training group, I attended a Life-in-the-Spirit Seminar offered by a Catholic Charismatic/Ecumenical Prayer Group. Through that seminar, I came to identify and experience the Holy Spirit.

After a powerful weekend experience, where "hands were laid" on me for the "stirring up" of the Gift of the Holy

Spirit,[4] Jesus truly came alive in my life. I've heard that experience makes a person aware of "new life," and that's what happened to me as well. I was "on fire," and I sought for the things of God through the Bible, teachings from others, and prayer. I felt more directed by the power of the Holy Spirit in personal prayer and in psychotherapy treatment with clients.

At this point in my professional life, I was an adjunct instructor in Mental Health Technology and Psychology at a community college, and—though Presbyterian—I was Supervisor of Catholic Social Services. I felt blessed to have the freedom to recognize the spiritual dimension and pray, as appropriate, with permission from the agency as well as clients.

After several months of trainings with the local group, I received an invitation to interview for a psychotherapy position with their practice, The Cornerstone. After accepting the position, I had an opportunity to offer psychotherapy treatment using a Christian/Catholic approach to healing. This differed from a materialistic and humanistic view of the human person. I could view the person from a Christian perspective, expanding into the relational division.

I joined the Association of Christian Therapists, which started as a multi-disciplinary Catholic charismatic, healing organization but became ecumenical soon after its inception. In 2014, the name changed to ACTHeals.org. When I became an active member, I was trained further in the integration of my Christian and Catholic faith into clinical work. I learned much about an interdisciplinary approach taught through Fr. Louis Lussier, O.S. Cam., MD, Ph.D., and other Christian/Catholic healthcare providers, and how to incorporate the spiritual dimension into an integrated treatment approach.

Fr. Lou was a key figure in the Association of Christian Therapists and influential, as he taught me about the human person. His work *Christian Anthropology of Healing: A Spiritual/Theological Perspective*[5] was especially helpful.

If some issues involving wounding manifested in physical (or somatic) symptoms, the first dimension of a holistic approach, these could be acknowledged with their effects on the psychological, relational, and spiritual dimensions. If a psychological problem (the second dimension) was the chief complaint, I could investigate the physical outbreak or the spiritual dimension (the third component).

Going deeper in matters with God involving anger, disappointment, sadness, etc., often freed the person psychologically and physically. Psychology was certainly bolstered by viewing and acting upon the importance of the spiritual dimension in a holistic viewpoint toward wounding and healing.

Fr. Lou writes:

The burden of sin, of our wounds and our wounding

others, carried in our body, soul, and spirit, affect our journey and response to God's invitation. This heavy burden results in disease and illness, in wounds and scars in our psyche and in our relationships, in confusion and loss of identity, in spiritual matters.

...To be cleansed and freed from this death we carry, we draw from what God inscribed as healing principles within our nature: physical, mental, emotional, and spiritual movements and mechanisms toward health and wholeness.[6]

In my recognition of a holistic and Christian approach to diagnosis and treatment, I prayed more—for my clients before, during, and after sessions and in my personal life. Much to my surprise and those who knew me well, I began to look like those in that initial psychotherapy training group—I prayed about everything! Was I becoming what some would consider a "radical"?

Thomas Dubay, in *Prayer Primer,*[7] says, "Prayer is a precious privilege—and this is putting it mildly. That the Lord of glory, himself unending joy, beauty, and goodness, would invite us to communicate with him and then begin the conversation with his inspired word, which welcomes our responses, is an unimaginable blessing."

And what a "precious privilege," truly a gift for me as a

therapist. I could listen to the Holy Spirit, in his gift of com-
munication, and find a better way with each client. Suddenly,
I was tapping into this gift every day in my office. Clients ap-
preciated in-session prayer, and for those who did not, I
didn't offer it. I once had a Jewish client who presented with
marital problems. He wanted me to pray with him, and I
tried to pray his way, without including Jesus Christ, but it
was difficult. Fortunately, he insisted that I pray instead as a
Christian, so I prayed to Jesus, and we were both happy.

Ruth Burrows, O.C.D., in her book, *The Essence of Prayer*
wrote:

> ….but a life that is truly Christian is all prayers. For
> God's 'chosen,' life is an unceasing desire expressed in
> their practical choosing of the divine will in all that hap-
> pens.
>
> It is a *being there* for God's coming in all the details
> of life, loving, purifying, transforming.[8]

Fr. Larry Richards, in his book, *Surrender: The Life-
Changing Power of Doing God's Will*, wrote that "prayer is
the secret of all the saints!"[9] He said if you want to know God
and live his will, then the one thing you must do is pray.

Fr. Larry spoke of preaching at a men's conference and
the speaker before him admonished the persons to pray each
day, no matter how busy they were. But Fr. Larry approached
it differently. He got up and said: "Gentlemen, you've got

two choices: You pray every day, or you go to hell." He said further, "Praying is more important than breathing. It needs to be a regular habit in all lives."[10]

In my practice, each client hour, the Holy Spirit truly became my "co-therapist," in his scriptural role as "Advocate" (See the Gospel of John, chapter 16).

Frequently, I contacted the Holy Spirit with an "SOS." I asked urgently and the Holy Spirit gave me direction and God's will for the client. My question was always: "How did Jesus want to bring his healing love to the client?" I knew that it was *his love that healed* and that if I could get in touch with the Heart of Jesus and his words, I would have the wisdom and understanding needed—not mine, but his.

† † †

Jason Evert in his book *St. John Paul the Great: His Five Loves* wrote that from his childhood, Karol (St. John Paul II) had a strong devotion to the Holy Spirit. He remembered his father telling him: "You don't pray to the Holy Spirit enough. You ought to pray to him."[11] His father gave him a prayer book on the Holy Spirit which was useful to John Paul II his whole life. He prayed every day for the gifts of the Holy Spirit. His prayer daily was:

Holy Spirit, I ask you for the gift of wisdom to better

know you and your divine perfections, for the gift of un-derstanding to clearly discern the spirit of the mysteries of the holy faith, for the gift of counsel that I may live according to the principles of this faith...[12]

When I think further about the importance of a regular prayer life—personally as well as professionally—and the leading of the Holy Spirit, I recall an example of a prayer life as demonstrated by a very holy, non-denominational pastor.

I was consulting with him about an ecumenical city-wide prayer meeting we were planning, and in one of those meet-ings, he demonstrated the importance and priority of prayer. I observed that he had a stack of 3x5 note cards in the pocket of his shirt. I was curious and asked: "What are the notecards for in your pocket?"

He told me that he arose early each morning and prayed about three hours before he went on the "missions" God had for him that day. He kept blank note cards in his pocket, so that he could record what the Holy Spirit of God said to him at any time of the day, so he got his directions and could act for God.

Wow, this was another dimension of prayer that the Holy Spirit revealed to me! He showed me through the pas-tor's priority of persistent listening that God wanted my at-tention not just at the start of the day, *all* day. I now knew I could bring Jesus' healing love approach to treatment.

Nicholas Herman was a young soldier who was raised in France in the 1600s and was religiously inclined as a young man. In 1635, he fought against Swedish infantry and French cavalry at Rambervillers, not far from his home village. He received a serious wound that left him with a limp which persisted his whole life. He had experienced many horrors in war, and he decided not to look back, but continue to look forward in his faith.

In 1640, he asked for admission to the Discalced Carmelites as a working brother, and he found a place in the community. After much struggle, he finally resigned himself to the mercy of God and learned to recognize God's presence in every aspect of his life. He prayed at all times, even in his tasks in the kitchen and in his community. He remained there for the next 50 years with the religious name of Brother Lawrence of the Resurrection.

It is said that he not only contemplated God in everything he saw, but also in everything that happened "he would raise himself up, going from the creature to the Creator."[13] He used the "visible" things he saw to get to the "invisible" God.

His approach was outlined in the book *Brother Lawrence of the Resurrection: Writings and Conversations on the Practice of the Presence of God:*

The holiest and most necessary practice in the spiritual life is that of the presence of God. It consists in taking delight in and becoming accustomed to his divine company, speaking humbly and conversing lovingly with him all the time, at every moment, without rule or measure; especially in times of temptation, suffering, aridity, weariness even infidelity and sin….

During our work and other activities, even during our reading, no matter how spiritual, and even during our religious exercises and vocal prayers, we must stop for a moment, as often as possible, to adore God in the depths of our hearts, to savor him even though in passing and on the sly, to praise him, to ask for his help, to offer him our hearts and to thank him. [14]

What an example of humility of a soul of one of God's creatures, who asked for help when needed, saw God in everything and gave thanks. His companioning of God throughout the day offers a powerful model of a daily life of prayer.

I converted to the faith in 1983 (that story later), and in 1992, I joined a Discalced Carmelite group. Like Brother Lawrence, I became immersed in prayer daily through the Carmelite's "Rule of Life." It consists also of several forms of mental prayer including meditation and contemplation.

As I continued to ponder that third question, "What is prayer?" my mind and heart were filled morning to evening with the practice of prayer, practicing the presence of God. I began the day with the *Liturgy of the Hours* morning prayer, meditative and contemplative prayer, rosary, and intercessory prayer for others, and finished the day with the *Liturgy of the Hours*, Chaplet of Divine Mercy, evening prayers and other personal prayers.

My conversion to Catholicism—explained more in depth later—came as a surprise to many of my family members and friends, but I truly felt it was a "call" from Jesus and the Blessed Mother. I began attending weekday Mass, the highest form of prayer, as well as enjoying periods of Eucharistic Adoration. On Sunday evenings, I also attended an ecumenical prayer group and prayed on a healing team for physical and inner healing for others.

† † †

St. Teresa of Jesus (Avila) is a Doctor of the Church, and her writings are very influential in the formation of prayer in the lives of many saints. In *The Interior Castle*, she writes of the soul and the seven stages of prayer through which the soul enters to obtain mystical union with God (I provide more about her seven "dwellings" in chapter seven).

In his book *Fulfillment of All Desire*, Ralph Martin explains that in St. Teresa's journey to full union with God, the objective is not the experience but in the conformity of our will with that of God's will, "in love of God and neighbor."

He added that God's will for us is our perfection, our total conformity to the love of God and neighbor.[15]

St. John Paul II the Great was also advanced in prayer. In his book, Jason Evert described him as persistent in prayer. He wrote:

> More remarkable than his daily, weekly, and annual traditions of prayer was his habit of incessant prayer. While walking from place to place inside the Vatican or outside, prayer became as natural and vital to him "as his breath."[16]

Evert also wrote that Archbishop Mieczyslaw Mokrzycki commented, "We knew we were not supposed to disturb the Holy Father then [when he was walking] because he was with God."[17]

According to Evert, Cardinal Christoph Schönborn observed:

> The Holy Father looked as though he never stopped praying. I never saw anyone so constantly immersed in union with Christ and God, as though it were a permanent state that led him to submit everything he did unto the Lord's hands. His attentiveness to others, his gestures, words and readings—everything he did was bathed in prayer, like the great mystics.[18]

Fr. Jacques Philippe in his book *Time for God* writes that even in receiving the sacraments, we must have a life of prayer. Fr. Philippe writes:

...without a life of prayer even the sacraments will have only a limited effect. Yes, they will give us grace, but that grace will remain unfruitful in part because the 'good soil' it needs is missing. Why, for instance, are so many people who receive communion frequently not more holy? The reason often is that do not have a life of prayer.[19]

Pope Benedict XVI, in the opening of his book *A School of Prayer* states: " . . . let us learn to live our relationship with the Lord even more intensely, as if it were as a 'school of prayer.'"[20]

† † †

As I counsel, offer workshops, and teach classes, I hear people's problems related to prayer. Finding intimacy with God is often difficult. Many feel the call to prayer and try to respond, but they can't settle down or be quiet for long, so a regular prayer life seeking God's will seems impossible.

They need to be taught not to give up when they have problems in prayer. Learning to be quiet and focused in meditative or contemplative prayer is another level that brings fulfillment in prayer. Learning to make each day a means to live their relationship more intensively with God "as if it were a school of prayer" seems like an essential goal for true intimacy with God.

In *Prayer Primer*, Fr. Thomas Dubay, S.M. asks, "Why another book on prayer?"[21] One answer he gave was that God is touching more people now. I also believe this is true and that it's even more important in the times in which we live; intimacy with God is threatened more than ever from secular choices.

As Fr. Dubay suggested, God has touched me in a profound way through prayer. Now that I have learned and continue to learn and experience intimacy with God with great satisfaction, it's time to instruct in a kind of "school of prayer" through this book. Perhaps my journey will open new pathways of constancy and closeness for others, and inspire a new love relationship with God, who wants us to love him with all that we are and all that we have.

CHAPTER 2

Morning Prayers

Dear God: So far today, I've done all right. I haven't gossiped. I haven't lost my temper. I haven't been greedy, grumpy, nasty, selfish or overindulgent. I'm very thankful for that. But in a few minutes, God, I'm going to get out of bed, and from then on I'm probably going to need a lot more help.

(unknown author)

Although this "prayer" is funny, is it not true? The moment we jump out of bed, the day begins to "take off" and "life happens" and often, even unintentionally, something comes out of our mouths or across in our actions that is not of God.

Either through the weakness of the flesh, the influence of the evil one–or both–we can begin the day—without "giving it to the Lord." For some people that means turning on the television for the news or watching movies; starting household duties, or hurriedly leaving for work; going to the gym, etc. In fact, God's presence and God's will can quickly be set aside. And I have noticed that the evil one takes delight in our forgetting that all belongs to God.

At the beginning of my day, my attention can be diverted by daydreaming, or using my imagination to create novel ideas, such as writing another book chapter. Or I can get lost getting a few more texts out, before I go to Mass. Instead, I should be armoring myself for the battle against evil, as Ephesians 6 advises: "Put on the armor of God so that you may be able to stand firm against the tactics of the devil." A prayer asking for protection and the full armor of God is beautiful and effective.

In Hebrews 4:12, we read:

> Indeed, the word of God is living and effective, sharper than any two-edged sword, penetrating even between soul and spirit, joints and marrow, and able to discern reflections and thoughts of the heart.

In recent years, I was led to a prayer that puts a hold, so to speak, on the practice of the evil one who might want to tamper with my life or those I love. Although I recognize that as a lay person I do not have authority to cast demons out as the priest does; I am, however, given authority to bind and can petition our Blessed Mother or Jesus to drive out demons. In *Deliverance Prayers: For Use by the Laity*, we're told that even without priestly authority, we can do binding prayers that begin with, "In the Name of Jesus, I command the spirit of _____ to be bound or quieted."[1] This method of prayer at the beginning or end of the day and throughout the day is helpful.

† † †

I recently, watched a segment from "That Man Is You," a production for Paradisus Dei, and discovered that I had been remiss in not calling on the holy angels more often for their intercession, particularly my guardian angel and also St. Raphael for healing.

Although I seek our protector, St. Michael, every day, there is much more that God has provided for us... if we but call on this heavenly host (A good book on this is Dr. Scott Hahn's *Angels and Saints: A Biblical Guide to Friendship with God's Holy Ones*.)

Each one of us is blessed to have our own personal guardian angel. As a child, you may have been taught this and learned that he is there to serve as your protector and your guide. In Fr. John Horgan's book *His Angels at Our Side,* he states:

> The role of guardian angel begins with conception and continues to our death. The angel is our faithful companion; even if we fall into serious sin, the angel does not leave us, but continues to try to inspire us to turn back to God. He may do this interiorly by speaking to our heart, or he may do this through the assistance of

other people and the circumstances of our lives, especially if we've become hardened to inspiration.[2]

Isn't this comforting? Did you also know that we can pray every morning and give permission to our guardian angel to act on our behalf or on another's behalf? There is much to learn about the holy angels, including our guardian angel and St. Michael the Archangel, perhaps the most widely known. It is worth taking time to better understand their role; and then let the Lord direct you on which angels to call upon.

There are many stories that I could tell. And you probably have many of your own stories of how your guardian angel took care of you in one way or another. Reading about your guardian angel and the nine choirs of angels and their roles in the mystical body is important.

I have one story that happened before I knew who angels were. I was snow skiing with my family in West Virginia. On previous snow-skiing vacations, we had been to Colorado, where the slopes were wide; the slopes in this particular spot were narrow. My brother was near me; and as I was skiing down a steep, narrow slope, I felt something push me aside. I immediately identified this "something" as an angel. Now sitting on the ground, I looked at my ski boots and realized they were unbuckled. Had I continued down the slope, I would have likely had an accident since my boots were not secure.

I was very grateful, and the Holy Spirit enlightened me that it was my angel who protected me. Since coming to know more about the angels and their mission, I have incorporated the guardian angel prayer into my morning prayers. It's a simple one to memorize:

Angel of God, my guardian dear, to whom God's love commits me here, ever this day be at my side, to light and guard, to rule and guide. Amen.

† † †

What God wants for our day is an important question to ask. For example, after I do a morning prayer offering to the Lord, I often pause to see if I can sense how the Holy Spirit might be leading me that day. Scripture can also bring us into the answers to that question. Sometimes the behaviors upon arising, mentioned in the silly opening prayer, occur because we haven't asked God or remembered his Word in scripture.

Author and speaker Lisa Brenninkmeyer wrote the bible study *Fearless and Free: Experiencing Healing and Wholeness in Christ.*[3] She quotes Dr. Bob Schuchts, who said: "The extent to which truth enters our hearts is the extent to which we come fully alive."[4]

To think of coming "fully alive" in the morning and for the rest of the day is exciting. In her eleven-week study, there

is the recognition that the evil one wants to keep you wres-
tling with prayer. In order to safeguard your prayer and life,
she offers scriptures that bring truth, as Dr. Bob Schuchts
suggests, and formats them in a section of her study entitled:
"I Declares."

Memorizing a few of these scriptural "I Declares" can be
helpful in protecting us from the wiles of the evil one. By
committing them to memory, they will sink into your heart,
and you don't have to wait for the brain to engage first. The
enemy is constantly at work tempting us to minimize the importance of God in our lives or leave him out. We don't want
that to happen! A few of the "I Declares" that are powerful
and can stave off the evil one, bring truth, and keep us "fully
alive" are:[5]

> I declare that if I trust in you with all my heart and
> don't lean on my own understanding, you will
> make my path straight (Proverbs 3:5-6).
> I declare that God's plans for me are to prosper me
> and not harm me, to give me a hope and a future
> (Jeremiah 29:11).
> I declare that if I seek first your kingdom and right-
> eousness, then all the things I need will be given
> to me as well (Luke 12: 31).

As 1 John 4:4 tells us, "…for the one who is in you is
greater than the one who is in the world." And the Gospel of

John 3:30 follows closely: "He must increase; I must decrease." Using these scriptures as guides, I seek to recognize and increase the Lord's presence *within* at the beginning of my day, starting with the *Liturgy of the Hours* prayers. This is part of the Carmelite *Rule of Life*,[6] along with other prayers and practices, that I will share more about throughout this book.

According to author Ralph Martin,[7] St. Frances de Sales, a doctor of the church, taught that as soon as we awake, we should fix our attention on the Lord and ask for his help to live the day in a manner that is pleasing to him. The saint further instructs us to take a lot of time for personal prayer as early in the morning as we can.

In *Introduction to the Devout Life,* St. Frances de Sales, writes that we should give an hour to meditation and "if you can, let it be early in the morning, when your mind will be less encumbered, and fresh after the night's rest."[8]

This is especially true for me. Some of us are "morning people" and some are more "night people," which means our circadian rhythms are more one than the other. When I counsel or provide spiritual direction, I ask simply: "Are you a morning person or a night person?" They usually have a sense of one or the other and then I can direct them in the best concentrated prayer time, especially for meditative/contemplative prayer.

Another good one to memorize is Psalm 121:2, "My help comes from the Lord, the maker of heaven and earth." And verse five continues, "The Lord is your guardian, the Lord is your shade at your right hand." I like to think of the Lord being at my right hand first thing in the morning.

Our *Catholic Catechism* further teaches us to pray "today." It is in the *present* that we encounter him—not yesterday nor tomorrow, but *today*. "Oh, that today you would hear his voice. Do not harden your hearts..." (Psalm 95:7–8).

Dan Burke, author of *Into the Deep*,[9] said his youngest brother once asked him a very important question: "Dan, do you pray every day?" And when Dan replied: "Every day," his brother clarified, "Every, every, *every* day?" The elder Burke finally explained to his brother that it was not because he was holy that he prayed, but because he could not imagine himself living a life without God.

† † †

Often, the first prayers of the day for me are my renewals of consecration to the Blessed Mother and to St. Joseph.[10] The second prayer of the day is a protection prayer as noted above from Ephesians 6 or a prayer of protection from the book *Deliverance Prayers: For Use by the Laity*. It reads:

Jesus Christ, our Lord and God, I ask Thee to render all spirits impotent, paralyzed and ineffective in attempting to take revenge against any one of us, our families, friends, communities, those who pray for us and their family members or anyone associated with us. I ask Thee to bind and sever and cut off all evil spirits, all powers in the air, the water, the ground, the fire, the underground, all emissaries of the satanic headquarters. I ask Thee to bind in Thy blood all of their attributes, aspects and characteristics, all of their interactions, communications and deceitful games. I break any and all bonds, ties and attachments in the Name of the Father, and of the Son, and of the Holy Spirit. Amen. [11]

Then there is the *Liturgy of the Hours.* In praying the *Liturgy of the Hours,* commonly thought of as "the office," I am praying at somewhat fixed ranges of times with my Carmelite sisters and Catholics–including priests, deacons, religious and consecrated–all over the world. It is comforting, and yet a little overwhelming, to think that I am in such holy company praying the same prayers. When I am in a Carmelite gathering at meetings or retreats, I pray with the group in common prayer.

The "office" includes psalms, canticles, antiphons, Gospel readings, and intercessions. The feast days of the saints and other holy days are celebrated with readings, so the whole church calendar is available. It is especially comforting to pray with the saints and to have that daily liturgical calendar.

Christian Prayer: The Liturgy of the Hours[12] states:

> From ancient times the church has had the custom of celebrating each day the liturgy of the hours. In this way the Church fulfills the Lord's precept to pray without ceasing, as once offering its praise to God the Father interceding for the salvation of the world . . . .The witness of the early church teaches us that individual Christians devoted themselves to prayer at fixed times. Then in different places, the custom soon grew of assigning special times to common prayer, for example, the last hour of the day, when evening draws on and the lamp is lighted, or the first hour, when night draws to a close with the rising of the daystar. . . .
>
> In the course of time other hours came to be sanctified by common prayer. These were seen by the Fathers as foreshadowed in the Acts of the Apostles.

My practice is to pray the *Liturgy of the Hours* morning prayers as well as the evening prayers.

One summer, while in formation to become a Spiritual Director, I attended a two-week school at Our Lady of Divine

Providence House of Prayer in Clearwater, Florida. It's a rather intensive training, most days beginning at 8:30 in the morning and finishing around 9:00 at night. The attendees were given some free time one Saturday afternoon, and we were thrilled to be invited to visit the home of the Foundress of the school, which was located on the Gulf. That meant we could enjoy the beach for a few hours, and of course, study scriptures for the next day's meeting.

I had a car, so I invited some religious sisters attending the school to ride with me. Loaded down with our bibles, journals, and Divine Office/breviaries, we set off, clearly in the mood for having fun.

Once in the car, one of the sisters asked if we could pray the *Liturgy of the Hours* together, which was their Rule and practice. What a scene! We had the windows rolled down, and these young sisters were in abbreviated clothing, so they could enjoy the beach. We were reciting the prayers of *Liturgy of the Hours* aloud, and I have never experienced such fun praying the afternoon prayers. We were in good form by the time we hit the sand, all "prayed up" and ready for the beach, which meant for them, wading along the shoreline. These sisters were holy and hilariously fun!

Another important morning prayer is the rosary of the day: Joyful, Sorrowful, Glorious, or Luminous. It's customary that mysteries be assigned to certain days of the week, which was affirmed by St. John Paul II. As author Scott Hahn writes:

The Rosary works on a human level, because it engages the whole person. It involves our speech and our hearing. It occupies our mind and incites our emotions. It assigns a task to our fingertips, those sensitive organs of touch. . . .We want [Jesus] to fill up our senses. [13]

I find this very true in my prayer life, as I ask the Blessed Mother and St. Joseph, in addition to Jesus, to hear my petitions for others, the community, the world, and for myself, while meditating on the mysteries. I feel as if I am "dumping out my heart" for whoever needs our Mother's intercession. (In a later chapter, I'll tell more about Mary's role in salvation history: To Jesus through Mary.)

Intercession is not new—it's biblical. For instance, in his book *A School of Prayer: The Saints Show Us How to Pray,* Pope Benedict XVI relates the story of Moses as an "intercessor." [14] Although Moses was a mediator between God and Israel and gave the people God's words and taught the Israelites to live in accordance with God's word, he also did a lot by praying. He prayed for the Pharaoh (Exodus 8-10), and he asked the Lord to heal his sister Miriam who was afflicted with leprosy (Numbers 12: 9-13). He also prayed for the people who had rebelled (Numbers 14: 1-19), and he prayed when the poisonous serpents took over the people (Numbers 21: 4-9). And much more.

In seeking to intercede for others, I count on the Holy Spirit, as he interacts with the Blessed Mother, to show me for whom to pray and how to pray for them. This is a close and personal time with Mary, as she assists me in remembering those individuals who have physical, mental, or spiritual needs, as well as my concerns about the community and the world and her concerns, too.

Often a person will come to mind, who is not in my usual cadre of people with needs (relatives, friends, etc.), and I believe it's due to the intervention of the Blessed Mother or the Holy Spirit, so I will bring that person(s) needs to the rosary intentions.

This occurred recently when I was walking and praying the rosary one morning. In a sudden flash, a name "popped up" of someone in the church whom I did not know well, nor had I prayed for him previously. He had a complex medical condition. Later, I saw him in a social situation and related how his name came to me. After expressing his gratitude, he immediately shared his medical situation. This was helpful, so that I could pray more fully. This is how the Lord uses the Body of Christ to link with one another in times of need.

† † †

In one of her apparitions, Our Lady of Fatima told the children to pray daily for world peace. Praying for world peace as well as peace in our country is a priority for me, especially with the unrest and political tension here in America. I pray that division and wars will cease and that the peace of Jesus will enter all hearts, "Then the peace of God that surpasses all understanding will guard your hearts and minds in Christ Jesus." (Philippians 4:7)

A section in *The Catechism of the Catholic Church* entitled "In Communion with the Holy Mother of God," says this:

> Jesus, the only mediator, is the way of our prayer; Mary, his mother and ours, is wholly transparent to him; She "shows the way," and is herself "the Sign" of the way, according to the traditional iconography of East and West (*CCC*, 2674).

This offering of morning prayers, plus other morning prayers, set the day apart for the Lord. Morning prayers prepare my heart, and I like to think I am preparing my heart through the heart of the Blessed Mother, so that I am *disposed* for God.

For example, I like to surround myself with spiritual items to dispose myself for God. In our family room, we have a picture of the Sacred Heart of Jesus that I like very much. I often greet the Lord through that image, "Good morning, Jesus." In most rooms of the house now, we have religious and/or blessed items that often provide a means for pointing toward God.

Here is a morning prayer from St. Therese of the Child Jesus (Lisieux)–one of my favorite saints–that stands in stark contrast to the silly one that opened this chapter.

O my God! I offer Thee all my actions of this day for the intentions and for the glory of the sacred Heart of Jesus. I desire to sanctify every beat of my heart, my every thought, my simplest works, by uniting them to Its infinite merits; and I wish to make reparation for my sins by casting them into the furnace of Its Merciful Love.

O my God! I ask of Thee for myself and for those whom I hold dear, the grace to fulfill perfectly Thy Holy Will, to accept for love Thee the joys and sorrows of this passing life, so that we may be one day united together in heaven for all Eternity. Amen. [15]

Here is another morning prayer that I use to ask for help through the Blessed Mother as she directs me to Jesus.

O Jesus, through the Immaculate Heart of Mary, I offer you my prayers, works, joys, and sufferings of this day, for all the intentions of your Sacred Heart, in union with the Holy Sacrifice of the Mass throughout the world, in reparation for sin, for the intentions of all my friends and associates, and in particular for the intentions of the Holy Father. Amen. [16]

When I think of praying through Mary's Immaculate Heart to Jesus as a devotion, I think of St. John Eudes, who so prominently brought people to love Christ and Mary by speaking continually about their hearts, the sign of the love God shows for us. The devotion to Mary's heart is concerned with the love of her heart for Jesus and for God. She shows us how to love God. And in later apparitions at Fatima, Mary asked for the establishment of devotion to her Immaculate Heart as a way to save the world.

I am asking that her heart of joys and sorrows, her virtues and hidden perfections, her virginal love for God and maternal love for her Son, and her compassion for all her children be with me. As she prays with me and for me, I am filled with the Lord's goodness and his mercy through her; and I am focused on what Jesus wants for me as he begins the day with me (and I with him).

Our Blessed Mother's appearance in Fatima (Portugal) was heralded in three appearances in 1916 by an angel who prepared the children for the Blessed Mother's visits. The Angel of Peace taught the visionaries two prayers[17] which I like to pray, from the heart, in the morning and several times throughout the day. I give more details about these prayers in Chapter 9, which is about the Blessed Mother. These prayers are for souls who need saving and prayers for the offenses against Jesus in the tabernacle and in the Eucharist. The Angel of Peace instructed the children to pray these prayers often throughout the day, so I also follow that instruction.

In 1989, I visited Medjugorje–which at the time was Yugoslavia. The Blessed Mother began appearing to six children there in 1981, and she has continued to appear to the visionaries into adulthood; four at the present time. During our visit there, we heard repeatedly that what mattered most was not the number of prayers that you prayed but that you prayed "from the heart."

In his book *Pray with the Heart! Medjugorje Manual of Prayer,* Fr. Slavko Barbaric, O.F.M. writes:

> When you come to Medjugorje, you will hear that we are called to prayer, not only to the one in the morning or evening, to the individual or common prayer, but the prayer with the heart as well. Every prayer can be finished in haste, so that we say all our prayers to the end, without having met Jesus and Mary. If we go on like this, there is a danger of our having only wasted our time, never coming to like prayer. Therefore, it is important to find time for prayer.[18]

"Meeting" Jesus and Mary is an important distinction, instead of "rushing through" to get the prayer finished. Or perhaps a person praying might not actually be ready to "sit." When I am making decisions, my spiritual director often asks, "Have you sat with Jesus and Mary?"

"Sit" is a verb that implies being in place, disposed to pray and hearing. According to the Webster's Dictionary, definitions that are particularly fitting are: to put in place; set in readiness; to give a tendency to; incline.

Before I "sit" with Jesus and Mary, I first want to pray to St. Joseph, the spouse of Mary and a wonderful, adopted father to us all. Through morning prayers, I have developed a special place in my heart for him, as protector of the family and the home. I pray that St. Joseph will intercede for me and for my concerns especially around family.

I am finding that as I pay attention to St. Joseph each day, he is becoming a part of my family life, just as Mary and Jesus and perhaps the Carmelite saints as well. As we acquaint ourselves with him and invite him into our homes, just as we do with the Blessed Mother, he becomes a family member, so to speak. He is the patron saint of families.

As a member of the Discalced Carmelites, I know that our foundress, St. Teresa of Jesus (Avila), had a strong devotion to St. Joseph and named her first reformed convent after him.

† † †

In my morning prayer time, I am meeting Jesus in a physical place and continue to pray deeply: physically, mentally, and spiritually. It's helpful to have your own prayer "corner" or "closet" that you can inhabit apart from other areas of your house. For disposing ourselves for prayer can often "make or break" our time with the Lord. It is about dis-position as much as it is about time and place.

At times, I have placed myself in situations where I want to pray but don't have time or I push myself to get prayers finished. In these situations, I find that I can't pray from the heart and the time doesn't go well. Frustration sets in, and I recognize a need to arrange my prayer time to give him "my best" if I can. If I examine these lost times, I discover it's often been a question of choosing my "will" over my "desires." I may be tempted to "put off" prayer at the usual time, but my "will" has to supersede desire or my prayer may be lost for the day.

One prayer in which I am inclined is to pray daily for the Pope, cardinals, bishops, priests—especially those dear to me—consecrated and religious men and women, and dea-cons in the Catholic church. I try to remember those priests who may have had trouble in their spiritual lives and inter-cede for them, as well as the end to the divisions I see in churches. I do not take lightly the importance of praying for our shepherds and those in service to the Church, but I want to be sure I have time and energy for this type of prayer. For myself, I notice that these prayers run deep.

I have come to know many priests over the years through my connection in the Association of Christian Therapists (now ACTHeals), as well as in my many travels to spiritual conferences. I am aware of the challenges of the priesthood, yet most of all, I somehow understand how important these ordained men are to the Lord, to his will being done for the church on earth and the salvation of souls. Without the priests, there is no Eucharist, our chief sacrament, and no Confession.

The book *Chalice of Strength, Prayers for Priests*[19] states that the Church calls us to unite ourselves with Mary and offer prayers and sufferings especially for priests. The Lord said to Venerable Conchita of Mexico (1862-1937):

> I want to come again into this world in my priests. I want to renew the world by revealing Myself through the priests. I want to give My Church a powerful impulse in which I will pour out the Holy Spirit over my priests like a new Pentecost. [20]

My prayer in response to this urging is simple, based on the practice of my favorite Carmelite saint, St. Therese of the Child Jesus (Lisieux). In my morning prayer, and many times along with rosary prayers or Divine Mercy Chaplet, I pray for faithful and fervent priests, unfaithful and tepid priests, those who are ministering at home and those who are ministering on mission, for tempted priests, lonely and desolate priests, young priests, for dying priests and for the souls of priests in purgatory.

It's a good practice to pray for those who are dear to us and in our hearts: the priest who baptized you, who confirmed you, the priests who have absolved you from your sins, the priests at whose Masses you may have assisted or who gave you the Body and Blood of Christ, the priests who instructed or taught you, and the priests to whom you are indebted to in any other way. I always ask the Lord to keep them close to his heart and bless them in time and in eternity.

St. Therese said to her sister Celine:

> Let us live for souls…let us be apostles…let us save especially the souls of priests;….Let us pray, let us suffer for them, and on the last day, Jesus will be grateful. We shall give him souls. [21]

Another devotion I find meaningful and essential is praying for the poor and suffering souls in purgatory. While Protestant, I never heard of this devotion, as Protestants do not believe in purgatory.

Over the years, I adopted this devotion and pray most mornings for those in purgatory, focusing most especially on my relatives and my husband's relatives. I do believe that the prayers and holy Masses said for them, especially those offered in November and on Christmas day, will shorten their stay in purgatory. It is also a way that I can continue to honor my parents and relatives, whom the Lord has given to me. Occasionally, as I say the generic prayers, a specific name will come to mind, and I will understand the Lord's leading and pray for particularly for that person.

Many of these souls are not Catholic, so have not been to

Reconciliation in the Catholic church. Further, even the Catholics who went to Reconciliation (Confession) for forgiveness of sins may still need to have temporal punishment for venial sins and forgiven mortal sins. The concept of purgatory made sense to me even before I understood the theology of the doctrine. *How could persons enter Heaven with a soiled past?* Our God is a holy God.

In one of the Fatima apparitions, the Blessed Mother's attire appeared dark. The children asked her about this, and she said that someone had touched her and this was the sin left over. That alone says it all.

The *Catholic Catechism* reports that in the Councils of Florence and Trent, the church formulated the doctrine of faith on purgatory. There are also references in the Holy Scriptures that spoke of a cleansing fire.

> As for certain lesser faults, we must believe that, before the Final Judgment, there is a purifying fire. He who is truth says that whoever utters blasphemy against the Holy Spirit will be pardoned neither in this age nor in the age to come. From this sentence, we understand that certain offenses can be forgiven in this age, but certain others in the age to come (*CCC*, 1031).

Also, there is the scripture from 2 Maccabees that permits praying for the dead. "Therefore (Judas Maccabeus) made atonement for the dead, that they might be delivered from their sin." (2 Macc. 12:46). The church has offered prayers and especially Eucharistic sacrifice, so that they become purified and attain the beatific vision of God (*CCC*, 1032).

† † †

St. Padre Pio, who is known for his ministry on behalf of those in purgatory and for his mystical experiences, tells the story of a visitation from a soul in purgatory. One day, he was praying alone, and he opened his eyes and saw an old man standing in his cell. He could not imagine how someone could be in the room since the friary was locked at this time of night. He asked the man who he was. He responded with his name and that he had died in that same friary in 1908 in a certain cell when it was still a poorhouse. He fell asleep one night with a lighted cigar, and it burned the mattress and he suffocated and burned. He told Padre Pio that he was still in purgatory and needed a holy Mass to be freed. He further said that God had allowed him to come and ask for Padre Pio's help. Padre Pio told him he would celebrate a Mass the next day so that he could be free. The next day, the priest confirmed the soul's story and celebrated Mass for him.[22]

The prayer by St. Gertrude is one of the most famous prayers for souls in purgatory. She was a Benedictine nun and mystic who lived in the 13th century. According to tradition, the Lord promised her that 1,000 souls would be released from purgatory each time she said a specific prayer devoutly. Here is that prayer:

> Eternal Father, I offer Thee the Most Precious Blood of Thy Divine Son Jesus, in union with the masses said throughout the world today, for all the holy souls in purgatory, for sinners everywhere, for sinners in the universal church and those in my own home and within my family. Amen. [23]

Well, there you have it! Lots of prayers and this doesn't even include the individual novenas, which I may offer for specific situations.

Before going to daily Mass, my husband and I also have prayer time together, praying for our children and grandchildren, for those who are sick or need God's love, for the community, the church, and the world. This is an intimate and comforting time for us to be together with the Lord, and we must work to get this time, as we are both busy in the morning and also getting ready for Mass.

Which brings us to the Holy Eucharist. Of the seven Sacraments of the Catholic Church, the Holy Eucharist is "the source and summit of the Christian life." (*CCC*, 1324)

As the *Catechism of the Catholic Church, second edition,* states:

The Eucharist is the efficacious sign and sublime cause of that communion in the divine life and that unity of the People of God by which the Church is kept in being. It is the culmination both of God's action sanctifying the world in Christ and of the worship men offer to Christ and through him to the Father in the Holy Spirit (*CCC*, 1325).

As you listen closely in Mass to all the prayers, including the scriptures and then participate in the Holy Sacrifice of the Mass, you are enveloped in a spiritual world that has no equal. We are praying with the Blessed Mother, the angels, and the saints. What a privilege! And just to think that we can partake of this holy time of re-presenting of the Last Supper every single day at a Catholic church just about anywhere in the world. Jesus is present in the Eucharist, living and healing, as we consume him.

The "real presence" is defined in the *Catholic Catechism* in this way:

The unique true presence of Christ in the Eucharist under the species or appearances of bread and wine. The Church invites the faithful to deepen their faith in the real presence of Christ through adoration and communion at the Eucharistic liturgy, and through adoration outside its celebration. [24]

As Vinny Flynn wrote in the *7 Secrets of the Eucharist*, "The Eucharist is alive."[25] Flynn described how, in 1916, in preparation of the Blessed Mother's appearance in Fatima, the Angel of Peace appeared three times to Lucia, Jacinta, and Francisco. In the third visit the Angel came with the Eucharist suspended in the air, and he prostrated himself on the ground and had the children repeat the following prayer three times:

> Most holy Trinity, Father, Son, and Holy Spirit, I offer you the most precious Body, blood and divinity of Jesus Christ, present in all the tabernacles of the world, in reparation for the outrages, sacrifices and indifference with which He Himself is offended. And, through the infinite merits of his most Sacred Heart, and the Immaculate Heart of Mary, I beg of you the conversion of sinners.[26]

Flynn points out that the angel prostrated himself on the ground, yet we stand in line to receive. The author suggests that we don't need to throw ourselves on the ground when receiving the Eucharist, but interiorly we can be "prostrate in adoration of the living God in the Eucharist."[27]

What a truly beautiful way to honor Jesus alive–in the Eucharist. Receiving Jesus in the Eucharist is the most personal and most prayerful I can be when I take him not only into my body, but also into my heart. And for those times when we cannot receive the holy Eucharist due to illness or in more recent times such as the pandemic, we can make an act of Spiritual Communion, as suggested by Pope Francis. Many of the faithful recited the following by St. Alphonsus Maria de Liguori (language modernized):

"My Jesus, I believe that you are present in the Blessed Sacrament. I love you above all things and I desire to receive you into my soul. Since I cannot at this moment receive you sacramentally, come at least spiritually into my heart. I embrace you as though you were already there and unite myself wholly to you. Never permit me to be separated from you. Amen."[28]

I am grateful to have the opportunity to be with Jesus in the Eucharist as often as I can. Before I became Catholic, I did not know what I was missing. I had a difficult, two-year struggle to become Catholic that started after feeling restless in the Presbyterian church. I sat Sunday after Sunday in the church service, feeling empty, strange, and–most of all–guilty that I could not find God. It was a noticeable internal restlessness and I asked myself, "Where is God?" And further, "Is there something wrong with me?" I discovered finally that the Blessed Mother was calling me to deeper intimacy with her son, Jesus Christ, in the Catholic faith; and so, I took a big step. (I share the full story in a later chapter.)

After several months of instruction by the priest, the day

finally came when I was to receive the Eucharist for the first time. Never was I more convinced of the "real presence" than that day when I received my first holy communion. I did not expect, nor could I have anticipated, what happened. There was such an overpowering emotional and spiritual awareness that Jesus was alive and with me for the first time ever. He truly was "the bread come down from Heaven" and filled every need. I knew that the Holy Spirit, through the Blessed Mother, had called me to this day and to this new relationship with the living Christ.

As I attend daily as well as weekend Mass, and as I consume the Eucharist–the living God–I am aware of his healing touch as I pray, lifting up to him the needs of others and asking healing for many, including for myself. (Much has been written about the healings over the centuries with the Eucharist, but that will need to be saved for another book.) Many times, I ask for the graces and healings I might receive to go to others and to the holy souls in purgatory. It is a special prayer time, a time of "life."

In John 6:51 and 57-58, we read:

I am the living bread that came down from heaven; whoever eats this bread will live forever; and the bread that I will give is my flesh for the life of the world. . . . Just as the living Father sent me and I have life because of the Father, so also the one who feeds on me will have life because of me. This is the bread that came down from heaven. Unlike your ancestors who ate and still died, whoever eats this bread will live forever.

And, finally, from *St. Faustina's Diary:*

Oh, what awesome mysteries take place during Mass!...One day we will know what God is doing for us in each Mass, and what sort of gift He is preparing in it for us. Only His divine love could permit that such a gift be provided for us.[29]

CHAPTER 3

Charity of the Heart Through Prayer

Although most times I think of myself as a "charitable" person–giving to and caring for other people through prayer and other spiritual acts of mercy daily–what sometimes comes to mind are the times when I've been "uncharitable."

I recognize that there can be a certain spiritual pride in thinking of yourself as charitable, but I don't think we always recognize there can also be spiritual pride in viewing yourself as uncharitable. It's a conversation you might consider having with God.

I'll start by offering a quick story. This is a story of *inaction* rather than action and of *omission* rather than *commission* of prayer.

It was a beautiful sunny day in New Orleans. My daughter and I went to Mass on that Sunday, before I headed back to my home in Florida. In preparation for the six-hour drive, I crossed the street to a nearby convenience store to purchase snacks.

Out of the corner of my eye, I saw a black middle-aged man, whom I perceived to be homeless. I knew the look and the behaviors well. His eyes were not focused on anyone; he was dressed poorly, somewhat ungroomed, and was in a hurry to get out of the store with his small package, trying to get by without attracting attention.

Although I noticed the man, I clearly avoided looking at him, deciding rather to look the other way, even though he was coming toward me. I made no acknowledgment of his presence–no hello, no smile, no connection. Instead, I turned away.

Here I had just consumed the Eucharist minutes earlier, but I had already forgotten about "being Eucharist" for others. Instead, I was in a rush to get out of New Orleans and distracted thinking about the long drive home. God soon convicted me in my inaction—not taking time to care or considering that maybe a more charitable response could be a witness to others.

I regretted my *inaction* almost immediately and pondered it further on the drive home. Even though I did not say any words that were uncharitable, my inaction and body language (not speaking and turning away) were "uncharitable." Further, I did not consider asking God what to do in that situation or even pray for the man. My heart was in conflict in the encounter, and instead of praying, I did nothing.

In the book *I Thirst: Saint Therese of Lisieux and Mother*

Teresa of Calcutta, Jacques Gauthier quoted Mother St. Teresa of Calcutta as saying that loneliness and lack of love were the greatest sufferings. "For her love was a fruit always in season," he said.

In giving love at any minute, any hour, she quenched that love of Jesus. She wanted to quench this thirst by ministering to the poorest of the poor, as if she were touching Jesus. Her happiness was to help the most vulnerable people of society and to touch Jesus in caring for them."[1]

Going back to my encounter, you might wonder, "What is the big deal with the man in the store?" Or, "Why would you think this was an inaction, omission, or uncharitable? After all, you didn't take any *direct action* that was uncharitable."

It's true that I did not say anything directly that was unkind or deny a request from the man or gossip about him. And yes, technically, I was not connected to him in any physicality as a neighbor. And yet . . . was he not my neighbor? And was he not among the most vulnerable people of society that the Gospel urges us to care for?

And what about love? As Mother Teresa might say, love was not "in season" for me at that moment. I had not dignified him with even a look, and therefore, *I had not looked at Jesus.*

As I strive to be a faithful servant of the Lord, I must hold myself accountable. I adhere to the scriptures from the Book of Luke, titled "Vigilant and Faithful Servants."

> That servant who knew his master's will but did not make preparations nor act in accord with his will shall be beaten severely; and the servant who was ignorant of his master's will but acted in a way deserving of a severe beating shall be beaten only lightly.
>
> Much will be required of the person entrusted with much, and still more will be demanded of the person entrusted with more. (Luke 12:47-48)

I understood that more was also required of me, as I spent several years working with the homeless in my professional career.

I was not ignorant of the feelings of loneliness, disconnection, and shame that lurked in the shadows of their hearts and minds. And this population had touched my heart in such a significant way. Jesus also advocated for the "least of the least." I knew the scripture from Matthew 25:31-56, titled "The Judgment of the Nations," which follows several parables about what's expected. " . . . whatever you did for one of these least brothers of mine, you did for me."

Once I noticed the discord in my heart on several levels, I needed to address what was within and what was without. What was I to do with myself or with the man I saw? What did God want to teach me about myself or him?

St. Ignatius of Loyola taught how to track the interior movements of the heart and take the action to follow God. Fr. Tim Gallagher tells St. Ignatius' story in his book *The Discernment of Spirits: An Ignatian Guide for Everyday Living*.

Ignatius discovered about his heart movements quite by accident. He was recovering from wounds from his battle in Pamplona and alternated his time between reading material of a spiritual nature, *The Lives of the Saints*, and using his imagination to spin tales of chivalry and favor with the ladies. One day, he said, his "eyes were opened a little."

God used this time to speak to his heart and change his direction in life. It led Ignatius to give us a way to discern God's will in the moment as well as long term, through what he called "Discernment of Spirits." As Gallagher writes:

> Little by little he came to recognize the difference between the spirits that agitated him, one from the demon, the other from God.

Ignatius discovered the distinction when he thought of the worldly project versus the spiritual project. In the worldly project, he would feel delighted but then after a time, the delight would switch from "delighted" to "dry and discontented."

Focusing on the spiritual idea of modeling after the saints, Ignatius also felt delighted, but the delight evolved into "consoled, content, and happy." He could then make his decision to travel to Jerusalem.

As Ignatius learned more, he would decide either to reject what he called "the bad spirit" or to accept the "good spirit" from God. Being aware of the movements of the heart became the important first step in the Ignatius three-step paradigm of discernment: becoming aware, understanding, and acting to accept or reject.[2]

When I studied under Fr. Gallagher for my spiritual direction certification, he taught me to use the three-step paradigm in applying the rules in my own life and also to teach it. Making decisions for God's will then became surer.

For instance, if I notice that my heart is registering a disturbance, annoyance, or other emotions that are not peaceful, I can acknowledge, then pray and ask the Holy Spirit to reveal the issue for me.

I also recognize that I need the Heart of Jesus when my heart isn't in the right place. My heart can hold a judgment against another person, for an attitude or behavior. Perhaps I don't speak anything outright. However, these "holdings" can be justified with defenses and rationalizations, so they remain–often filling the heart.

What accumulates in the heart is a sort of self-love or pride. Whether there is an action or not, the heart stays blocked from love of God or love of another and stays instead focused on the self. The consequence can be an unloving and unbalanced decision.

In *The Dark Night: Psychological Experience and Spiritual Reality*, Fr. Marc Foley, O.C.D., addresses spiritual pride. There is a certain consolation that can come from an egocentric perspective about the good that we do or the opinion we hold of ourselves.

Using the work of St. John of the Cross as a background, Fr. Foley relates the story of Joe who became proficient in his spiritual journey by growing in the virtues, but then he began to pride himself on his ascetical achievements and had "a secret joy when he saw that so many of his peers lacked the self-discipline that he had acquired."

Fr. Foley said spiritual pride is "mercurial by nature; it assumes different forms and becomes harder to detect the more that it counterfeits virtue."[3]

That means I can ask Jesus to illuminate what is counterfeit. It's like putting the plug into the power source for the electricity, so that a light comes on. And I can ask for his cleansing.

A familiar scripture comes to mind, Psalm 51:12, "A clean heart create for me O God; renew within me a steadfast spirit."

Also, in Matthew 5, the sixth Beatitude is: "Blessed are the pure in heart, for they shall see God." The Beatitudes were given for "those ready to be set free by love and are for the Kingdom of Heaven."[4]

The *Catechism of the Catholic Church* addressed "Purification of the Heart" and charity in relation to the sixth Beatitude.

> "Pure in heart" refers to those who have attuned their intellects and wills to the demands of God's holiness, chiefly in three areas: charity, chastity or sexual rectitude, love of truth and orthodoxy of faith. There is a connection between purity of heart, of body, and of faith (*CCC*, 2518)

It's no small matter to attune our intellects and wills to be holy, so that there is a connection between "purity of heart, of body and of faith" that God wants for us. As my story illustrates, it requires effort to develop as well as recognition when we fail.

The story of St. Therese of the Child Jesus (Lisieux) is one that encourages additional help with purity of heart.

St. Therese decided that her vocation was love and that love, as defined by the scriptures (1 Corinthians 12: 31 and 1 Corinthians 13: 1-13), was "the more excellent way."

Her desire was to perform great deeds for God, however, she recognized limitations by her state of life. She knew she would not achieve deeds as extraordinary as St. Teresa of Jesus (Avila) or St. John of the Cross. However, she concluded, it was not the extraordinary that the Lord wanted, but, instead, he desired that each deed–no matter how small–be done in great love. The little sacrifices she made *were* the extraordinary deeds.

In a study guide version of St. Therese's autobiography *St. Therese of Lisieux: Story of a Soul,* Fr. Marc Foley[5] clarifies that it is not about just being nice. He says, "When we love with the love of charity, our actions are the actions of God."

St. Therese teaches us that our love for God is proven not out of our fervor and love for him, but when we act in a loving manner, even when we do not have the strength to be virtuous or do not have the courage, he said.

In her book, Therese is telling her sister, Celine, that when you get up in the morning and you don't feel like praying or don't feel like loving your neighbor, it is in these times that you prove your love for God because the love will come from the will alone and doesn't have to have the emotion with it.

I believe this is true and certainly worth much reflection. How often do we fail to have loving feelings for those we live with or have around us, perhaps discounting the importance of addressing these, and not identifying the sin? God wants us to have a heart like his, full of love, forgiveness, and mercy.

We should ask ourselves, "Do we strive for this or let this go?"

A few years ago, my husband and I decided to celebrate my birthday with friends at a restaurant, and we traveled by boat to get there. As was my custom, I intended to pray and ask the Lord for his birthday gift or a word from him. Taking my bible and other spiritual books on the boat, I looked forward to that time of prayer. But then I received a phone call from a former client who had a problem. After answering and hearing of the problem, I grew irritated. I thought to myself, "After all, it is my birthday." I queried God: "Couldn't I have rest from my counseling work on this *one* day?"

The answer became clear. In spite of my initial annoyance, I needed to give her my full attention; and I would do this from my will, as St. Therese suggested. I hoped that my former client could feel love and care, even if it was from my will alone.

Knowing that my heart was not peaceful, I prayed, and the Holy Spirit pointed me to John 21:15, when Jesus asked Peter: "Do you love me . . . ?" three times.

Peter answered "yes" all three times, and Jesus told him, "Feed my lambs," "Tend my sheep," and "Feed my sheep." And I sensed Jesus also saying to me: "Feed my sheep."

I felt humbled by the scripture and recognized it was the mercy of God. God wanted to meet this person's needs. He needed to use me, but first he had to humble me. Focusing on God's will for the person in God's timetable, rather than mine or on my own wants and needs, was a remarkable teaching for me.

Fortunately, I "got" this message, so when a second call came from that former client, I knew that God was giving me another opportunity to be loving and merciful. The scripture from John 21 as well as my humbling were God's birthday gifts to me, and I gratefully embraced them. My heart needed to change, to "love with the gift of charity." In this case, because I had taken time to pray, listen, and repent, my heart emotions underwent a change to be more charitable.

† † †

Therese teaches us to "love with the love of charity." In one letter to her sister, she wrote:

> . . . After I have committed a fault, even a slight one, my soul experiences a certain sadness or uneasiness for some little time. Then I tell myself, "Now little one, this is the price you must pay for your fault," and so I patiently bear with the trial until the little debt is paid.[6]

In his *Study Guide*, Fr. Foley interpreted that as Therese patiently carrying the pain of the fault and confiding herself to the mercy of God. And it is by the mercy of God only that she (and we) are purified.

The following quote made it clear for me. St. Therese writes: "In one act of love, even unfelt love, all is repaired and Jesus smiles."[7] So for me, it is about following a God who loves and who wants our hearts to love his creatures as he loves them. St. Ignatius would tell me to know the affectivity of my heart, and St. Therese would direct me to seek the mercy of God in that unfelt love.

In his book *The Way of Trust and Love,* Fr. Jacques Philippe said Therese learned about the deeper meaning of charity at the end of her life. Jesus asked her to love the people that she lived with every day, and he connected the first and second commandment for her. When you love your neighbor, you love God. It is easy to love the people far away and to pray for missionaries, much more difficult for us to love the ones next door.

So, it seems we must look to God first, through our wills, to pray, and allow him to work with our emotions to bring them into conformity with his will, which is love and mercy.

In Fr. Jacques Philippe's book *Time for God,* he writes that prayer can be a source of much fruitfulness for a person:

> It transforms us, sanctifies us, heals us, helps us to love and know God, makes us fervent and generous in love of neighbor.[8]

In writing of humility in another book on St. Therese, *The Way of Trust and Love,* Fr. Philippe says that if we are in right relation with ourselves, we can be in right relationship with God and also with others. By humbly accepting our limitations and weaknesses, we more easily get along with ourselves and then others. We can love others as they are, when we can love ourselves as we are.

One of the toughest situations in which to love and seek

his mercy through prayer is when our hearts are not loving, are uncharitable, and are filled with unforgiveness.

Fr. Richard McAlear, OMI, is considered by many as the "forgiveness priest." In his book *Forgiveness, New and Expanded Edition: Experiencing God's Mercy,* he says that Jesus gave us the gift of forgiveness from the Cross; his mission was about mercy. Not only does Jesus proclaim the grace of mercy, but he commands us to forgive, and further teaches about the dangers of unforgiveness in the heart. Fr. McAlear wrote that when we hold unforgiveness, we block the movement of the Holy Spirit; our spiritual life is blocked, and healing cannot flow.

† † †

Several years ago, I attended an out-of-town conference for psychotherapists. On the first day, I was approached by a lady from another town, whom I knew well, and she asked me to sit with her group. Since this invitation caught me by surprise, I didn't say "no" quickly enough. Unfortunately, this lady was well-known for causing a family breakup and, knowing the family well, I did not have charitable feelings toward her. So that first day I sat in much discomfort with her group and also had lunch with them.

At the end of that day, I determined that I would not join her group again. As I returned to the hotel that evening, I related the story to my husband and made a plan of how to avoid her.

I plotted and planned my arrival to be several minutes after the start of the next day's program, figuring that she and the group would have found seats already, not including me. I further invited my husband to meet me for lunch, to avoid her a second time during that day. And both plans worked!

But the question remained later for me: Did I have charity in my heart for this lady or not? What was going on interiorly? I determined it was not very pretty.

In his book *Interior Freedom*, Fr. Phillipe writes that when we hold unforgiveness, we "will always be prisoners of our own bitterness."[9] Our hearts are definitely not clean.

In his book *The Power of Healing Prayer: Overcoming Emotional and Psychological Blocks*, Fr. Richard McAlear wrote that as one is forgiven by God, we are to forgive others. Healing and forgiveness are intertwined as resentment and anger can cause physical, emotional, and psychological problems. In addition, he found that some people became sick physically as they carried grudges and sought revenge.

Unforgiveness stands as a barrier to the healing power and forgiving love of God. That obstacle can be removed only with a decision to love.[10]

And the will of God is clear in Luke 6:27-35:

"But to you who hear I say, love your enemies, do good to those who hate you, bless those who curse you, pray for those who mistreat you. To the person who strikes you on one cheek, offer the other one as well, and from the person who takes your cloak, do not withhold even your tunic. Give to everyone who asks of you, and from the one who takes what is yours do not demand it back.

Do to others as you would have them do to you. For if you love those who love you, what credit is that to you? Even sinners love those who love them.

And if you do good to those who do good to you, what credit is that to you? Even sinners do the same.

If you lend money to those from whom you expect repayment, what credit [is] that to you? Even sinners lend to sinners and get back the same amount.

But rather, love your enemies and do good to them, and lend expecting nothing back; then your reward will be great ..."

† † †

I did not feel particularly good about my heart stirrings, as well as my actions at the conference. For two days, while pondering my pre-meditated plan of avoidance, I felt anger, unforgiveness and negativity toward the woman, as well as toward myself.

Consequently, I looked forward to a telephone call with my spiritual director, a Jesuit priest. He had advised me, early in our direction that I should not tell him about my "successes," but rather about my "humiliations."

So, here was a big one! I couldn't wait to tell him about this latest humiliation. Although he listened carefully and compassionately, he questioned, and my heart sank when he asked: "Did you ask Jesus what to do?" I reluctantly told him the truth: "No, I did not ask Jesus what to do." He followed up by asking "Why not?"

I could offer no answer or excuse. My spiritual director was clear, saying that Jesus might have had a different plan for me in my contact with the lady. Although he did not confront me directly about my unforgiveness, upon hearing his response, I was again filled with remorse. His observation gave me further insight—that I had not prayed to ask the Lord what his will would be before I made the decision, based on my own will.

My heart was not clean at the time that my pre-meditated plan was developing, and because I did not pray, I did not give Jesus an opportunity for my transformation.

The lessons learned from this painful experience were not lost. I now regularly ask Jesus what to do in most situations, particularly as I notice my heart stirrings. I can do a self-check by asking, *Is there peace in my heart or not?*

This is a good question to use as a quick mental or spiritual check throughout the day.

† † †

My experiences with persons and couples in psychotherapy alerted me to the presence of being not at peace, but instead having resentments—sometimes little and sometimes big—that were often let go by unnoticed.

Resentment, I discovered, is different from anger—which is a spontaneous emotion that arises quickly and then goes away just as quickly. Resentments have the character of vengeance or a grudge.

Years ago, a well-known psychiatric nurse, former president of ACT, consultant and trainer, Dr. Margarett Schlientz, gave a beautiful keynote presentation on resentments at an international ACT conference I attended. The talk has remained with me and influenced my therapeutic work. To paraphrase, she said that resentment was like a slow-burning coal. It stays underneath, so sometimes we don't notice, until some big issue hits. And suddenly, emotion can be like a volcano spilling over.

Understanding this concept intellectually and trying to monitor my own resentments from forming, plus noticing this in my therapy clients, led me to focus more and more on forgiveness as a therapeutic and spiritual solution. My goal is to help people resolve their issues within themselves or between them. However, an issue not as commonly noticed or understood, but often underneath with people of faith is "Where was God in all this?" and "Why did you allow this to happen (God)?"

In his book *Forgiveness: Experiencing God's Mercy*, Fr. Richard McAlear wrote that sometimes persons will not want to face God and admit any resentment to him. But if they don't face the issue, deeper conflicts will remain. Hurts and disappointments with God, unresolved, will show up another way.[11]

To understand the resentment couples had, which blocked them from loving one another, I would suggest to couples that they query between them what they were grateful for or ungrateful for at the end of each day. Obviously, the ungratefulness was an area that needed forgiveness. Learning to apologize and say, "I'm sorry," without excuses, is another work in the process of forgiveness. In my doctoral dissertation, entitled *The Clinical Use of Forgiveness in Marital Group Therapy*, I researched forgiveness and mercy and ran a marital group with a co-worker in my practice. In the group, we integrated the clinical as well as spiritual components and benefits of forgiveness.

I have learned from my own experiences, especially with relatives, how to put myself in a humble position and reflect with Jesus, in order to reveal and acknowledge my insensitivity or wrongdoing. I now know and teach how to help the person get over the hurt by a few well-meaning, heart-felt words that may need to be repeated: "I'm sorry," "I didn't mean to hurt you," "There is no excuse." And most important to be followed with a question: "Will you forgive me?"

If you haven't done this before, it may be uncomfortable. You must experience the person's hurt fully without defending yourself, which is not easy.

† † †

Chicken Soup for the Christian Soul includes a beautiful story of Corrie Ten Boom. Her book *The Hiding Place* was very inspirational in recounting the story of her life with her sister in Ravensbruck, a Nazi detention camp.

As the story goes, Corrie was giving a talk on forgiveness in a church in Munich in 1947. She said it was usually silent after these talks in Germany, but in this particular church a man came up to her, whom she recognized. She remembered his uniform, as he had been a guard at Ravensbruck, where she and her sister Betsy were kept, and where Betsy died. It was one of the cruelest of the camps.

The man revealed to Corrie that he had been a guard but had since become a Christian. He knew that God had forgiven him, but he now wanted her forgiveness (as a prisoner), though he did not remember ever meeting Corrie or her sister.

He said, "Will you forgive me?" She froze and did not think she could forgive him, but directed herself inward:

> I knew it not only as a commandment of God, but as a daily experience. Those who were able to forgive their former enemies were able to return to the outside world and rebuild their lives, no matter what the physical scars. Those who nursed their bitterness remained invalids. [12]

She knew that forgiveness was an act of the will, rather than feelings, and that the act of the will could change the heart. So, she prayed silently that Jesus would help with the feeling. The guard was standing in front of her with his hand extended, but she was having difficulty responding. She finally put her hand into his and immediately felt a current down her arm. She told the man that she forgave him from her heart; and later recalled the interior movement—she had never known such an intense love.

I wonder if Corrie would have had the strength or the courage to extend her hand and to say the words of forgiveness had she not prayed and then moved into her will. She knew the scriptures. She did what she knew was the instruction by the Lord, even when her heart was not in a good place.

Even in a quick prayer, as Mother St. Teresa of Calcutta reminds us, all is repaired and Jesus smiles.

Jesus teaches us a way of love and mercy—of charity, not just in our actions, but in our hearts. He gives us a model of how to seek him in prayer and ask the power of the Holy Spirit to instruct us and remind us of all that he has taught. Jesus prayed in all situations, and his heart was filled with compassion, understanding the Father's will for him.

In Fr. Philippe's book *Interior Freedom*, he says "Needing to feel secure, we would like always to be sure of doing God's will."[13] He writes of the normality of this desire and yet "if we seek God's will with a sincere heart, we will receive the light to understand it."[14]

He writes as much as we seek God's will, we may not get the answer as clearly as we wish it at that moment, but it will come later. God treats us as adults, in many situations, and wants us to use our intellect and discernment; and he wants purification. "Not always being absolutely sure we are doing God's will is humbling and painful, but protects us." This way we are always seeking, and it keeps us from a false security. He says we must keep abandoning ourselves to God.

† † †

While riding a train in 1946 on the way to her annual retreat, Mother St. Teresa of Calcutta prayed. She called this her "Day of Inspiration," as she felt that the Holy Spirit inspired her. She felt Jesus' immense thirst for love. Within her, she felt the call to serve the poorest of the poor, as these were the most precious people to Jesus. She consecrated her life, and it was an order from God to serve and live among the poor. She wanted to quench his thirst. As Mother Teresa wrote:

> The message was quite clear I was to leave the convent and consecrate myself completely to serve the poor, and live among them. It was an order, I knew where I belonged but I did not know how to get there.

As we know, she went on to establish the Missionaries of Charity. The foundation of St. Teresa of Calcutta's work was prayer for strength in trials and as an expression of joy. Her tools were silent prayer, adoration before the Blessed Sacrament, the liturgy, and the rosary. In *No Greater Love*, she writes: "Prayer enlarges the heart until it is capable of containing God's gift of himself." [15]

God gives us the opportunity to pray to seek him and do his will, so that we can grow more and more in his image, that image of love, mercy, and forgiveness. God's gift to us is growing more like him—if we humble ourselves before him, listen, and follow as he leads us into the depths of his heart, which is charity itself.

Will we allow our hearts to grow in love and seek the one who *is* Love, to teach us through prayer?

CHAPTER 4

Eucharistic Adoration and Prayer

When I initially became Catholic, I scarcely knew how to sit still or keep my eyes closed in prayer for ten minutes. At that time, prayer for me was not listening to God, but talking. My petitions were endless: I asked for everything and didn't give God a chance to respond before I was off to the races with another petition.

Although petitioning God in itself is not bad, Jesus tells us in Matthew 7:7-8:

> Ask and it will be given to you; seek and you will find; knock and the door will be opened to you. For everyone who asks, receives; and the one who seeks finds; and to the one who knocks, the door will be opened.

This tells me that we ask in confidence and leave room for the "receiving" part. That is done quietly in his time, and we need to leave room for it. But silence, initially, was daunting for me.

So, imagine my surprise when the speaker at a Catholic conference I attended in Estes Park, Colorado, announced, "I am not going to speak to you today about contemplation, but instead we will have Eucharistic Adoration." And Eucharistic Adoration required silence for a lot longer than ten minutes!

So, here I was a "baby" Catholic, and former Presbyterian who knew nothing of this type of prayer, about to adore Jesus in silence for a full hour. Fortunately, I had my devout Catholic friend with me for instructions and encouragement.

Into the silence I entered—and into the mystery of knowing Jesus in the exposition of the Blessed Sacrament. As I respected the external quiet, I also became quiet within. This new kind of internal quiet was amazing. I was further stunned when I had a vision in my mind's eye, a first for me. I saw a skeleton hand, which appeared consumed with leprosy. Although I understood to some extent about visions, I did not know God's intent with this particular image. And I also wondered, *Why me?*

We were sitting high up in the auditorium, but silently my friend motioned me to follow her onto the conference floor. Once there, she showed me how to lie prostrate in front of the monstrance with Jesus, the Blessed Sacrament. She very reverently whispered instructions and assured me that it was normal to adore Jesus in this manner. It was unfamiliar and I was a bit overwhelmed, but I managed to remain very still, along with her and others who were on the floor.

As I found myself in proximity to Jesus, exposed from the Tabernacle, I was aware that this was a holy thing to do, but unsure of what to expect or do next. I soon discovered that there was no expectation, nothing to "do," except surrender to him in the moment in his "living" presence. I say "living" as this was a consecrated host, that through the consecration had become "the body and blood of Christ." Surrendering meant quieting myself externally and internally and waiting. (I later discovered that I was waiting on the Holy Spirit to move me.)

We stayed on the floor for many minutes it seemed, worshipping face down. Then, suddenly, I felt the presence of Jesus enveloping me. It was an intimate moment, and I was aware of nothing else in the conference hall, but him. Time seemed to stop, and that moment was all that mattered.

I equated this awe-filled experience to my first reception of the Holy Eucharist the previous year, when I became a confirmed Catholic. As I received the Eucharist for the first time, I knew within every fiber of my body that Jesus was real and living now—at that moment and in our time—and better yet, he wanted a personal relationship with me. I bonded to him in his living presence, as Savior and Lord.

I later realized that the Holy Spirit directed me to that moment of my first communion. He wanted me to participate in the Catholic faith and to experience the truth of Jesus' living presence in the Eucharist.

Now as I lay prostrate in front of the monstrance, Jesus was connecting to me and I to him; and I will never forget this second moment of attachment, which even today warms and sustains me.

At the finish of Eucharistic Adoration, my friend and I shared the visions given to us by the Lord. Her vision, considered an infused contemplation,[1] was a beautiful, splendid vision of the Blessed Mother, unlike any she had been given before.

She was so amazed with its brilliance, she shared it with one of the founders of the organization for interpretation. Many years later, she related to me that the vision was so overpowering still, and she lacked full comprehension to this day.

I did not know then what I know now about visions, healings, and transformations that could occur during private Eucharistic Adoration.

We know from scripture that Jesus is the "bread of life." In John 6:32-35 we read:

> Jesus then said to them, "Truly, truly, I say to you, it was not Moses who gave you the bread from heaven; my Father gives you the true bread from heaven. For the bread of God is that which came down from heaven, and gives life to the world." They said to him, "Lord, give us this bread always." Jesus said to them, "I am the bread of life; he who comes to me shall not hunger, and he who believes in me shall never thirst." (*New American Bible, St. Joseph edition*)

In the *Catechism of the Catholic Church, we read*:

> Since Christ was about to take his departure from his own in his visible form, he wanted to give us his sacramental presence; since he was about to offer himself on the cross to save us 'to the end,' even to the giving of his life. In his Eucharistic presence he remains mysteriously in our midst as the one who loved us and gave himself up for us, and he remains under signs that express and communicate this love. (*CCC*, 1380)

The importance of Eucharist Adoration is shown in the fact that the Church has a ritual that regulates it: *The Rite of Eucharistic Exposition and Benediction*. This is an extension of the Adoration of the Blessed Sacrament which occurs in every Mass as the priest says: "Behold the Lamb of God, behold him who takes away the sins of the world. Blessed are those called to the supper of the Lamb."

Exposition of the Blessed Sacrament flows from the sacrifice of the Mass and serves to deepen our hunger for communion with Christ and the rest of the Church. The Rite concludes with the ordained minister offering a "benediction" or blessing of the faithful by lifting the monstrance containing the Blessed Sacrament.

When I began the regular practice of Eucharistic Adoration, I found discomfort in my silence and his. At first, I was distracted by details of recent activities, such as the work-shop just presented, the social event I attended with my husband, or client problems in relationships. The flood of thoughts kept me whirling in my own life, apart from God's.

There were the noises of others, too—the sound of shoes entering the Adoration Chapel, the blowing of noses, the rustling of papers, or the whisperings of the rosary. Feeling annoyed and unloving, after awhile, I would give up on my attempt to focus on God's love and leave the chapel.

Once, I had a particularly frustrating time in the Adoration Chapel. Confessing some things to a priest in Reconciliation, I decided at the last minute to tell him about my annoying experience in Adoration. A person was reading a secular book and making noises. In confessing to the priest, I imagined that he would be understanding and concur with my annoyance.

Interestingly, however, he took another approach and asked me to think about how happy God must have been that the person was there, even if he wasn't quiet or was reading secular material. Needless to say, after connecting with my own sinfulness, I felt humbled. What a lesson learned about God's redeeming love, unlike mine, that reaches and does not expect perfection, but is patient and kind, all those qualities we read in the definition of love found so beautifully in 1 Corinthians 13: 4-13. Another lesson of love learned in the confessional.

Today, unlike my first experience at the conference, or

first experiences in Adoration chapels, as I enter into his Living Presence, I am more comfortable, not as fearful or questioning, and certainly not as critical.

In spite of more comfort, restlessness may accompany me into the Adoration Chapel; and I often have to ask for more grace to settle down and experience Jesus within. He gives me "life," the "true bread" come down from heaven. Entering his silence and mine, praying, and gazing upon him in the gleaming, gold monstrance, I realize that there is no other relationship which nourishes and touches me as deeply.

I picture myself as similar to the lady who had the blood flow disease in the Gospel of John; and I imagine how she felt (Mark 5:30—34). As she approached Jesus from behind, she must have inwardly acknowledged her unworthiness.

But she was so focused on Jesus and her need for healing from suffering that had only grown worse for twelve years, that she braved a touch, trusting that healing would come forth. It took just a touch, and she was healed of her disease. Jesus said to her, "Daughter, your faith has saved you. Go in peace and be cured of your affliction." (Mark 5:34).

I now know that the encounters with him, however long or short, bring healing in body, soul, or spirit, whether I can identify specifically the source of healing or not. It goes out from him; of this, I can be sure.

† † †

In *The Discernment of Spirits: An Ignatian Guide to Everyday Living,* Fr. Tim Gallagher wrote of the historical wounds affecting our wholeness contained in biblical theology from Genesis 3. We have hurts that we don't want to see or face, along with lack of spiritual instruction and these keep us facing outward instead of inward.

Robert Cardinal Sarah in *The Power of Silence: Against the Dictatorship of Noise* writes:

> Too few Christians today are willing to go back inside themselves so as to look at themselves and let God look at them. I insist: too few are willing to confront God in silence, by coming to be burned in that great face-to-face encounter.[2]

In his book *Catechism on the Real Presence,*[3] Fr. John Hardon, S.J., writes that Pope Paul VI encouraged a daily visit to the Blessed Sacrament. The book is based on the encyclical letter *Mysterium Fidei,* published on September 3, 1965, by Pope Paul VI and issued during the session of the Second Vatican Council. Hardon said the Pope declared that such visits are at once a proof of our gratitude, an expression of our love and a profession of our faith in Christ's presence on earth.

When I am close to Jesus in Adoration, I can ask the Holy Spirit to help me "get past" the busyness of the morning and turn my attention inward to become still; and something changes interiorly. The more I keep my eyes on him outwardly in the monstrance, and inwardly in prayer in silence, I open myself to receive his love. It is like getting a new tank of gas. I am "filled up," and my words do not justly describe what I experience.

Perhaps Fr. Sean Davidson expresses my sentiments best with this quote from his book *Saint Mary Magdalene, Prophetess of Eucharistic Love*: "To the soul of an adorer, the Real Presence of Christ is like a fountain of living water in a dry and arid land."[4]

Looking forward to that hour spent with Jesus, I often begin with thanksgiving for the blessings of his Presence in the Eucharist. In *Miracle Hour,*[5] Linda Schubert offers an outline for an hour of prayer for a "rich, grace-filled hour" in five-minute segments, drawing one deeper into intimacy with Jesus. She begins with praise and singing to the Lord and finishes with thanksgiving in the twelfth segment. Her book is a pathway for any newcomer in prayer.

After some time in adoration, when I am calm and focused, I may ask a specific question of the Lord. I always have my journal, ready to record the reply. I can offer a few examples to illustrate.

I was attending daily Mass, not a usual practice in my earlier faith walk, and I asked the Lord if it was necessary for me to continue. I heard very clearly in my spirit. "It is in daily Mass where I will re-tool you."

Another time, I went to Adoration seeking his direction to whether to be involved in a new center for the homeless. Even though I was in the private practice of psychotherapy at the time, I had volunteered in the efforts for hurricane relief in the community, a project that was meaningful to me. My volunteer work was noticed, and I began to feel pressure from leadership.

I asked the Holy Spirit for a sign that I was to head the project. The Holy Spirit brought to my memory a book entitled *The Cross and the Switchblade* by David Wilkerson that I'd read long ago. It was about a pastor who, directed by God, left a mainline church to pastor an inner-city church. This story seemed significant as the pastor said "yes" to a very different ministry in a different geographic area. His choice seemed to parallel the one that I was being asked to make.

I sometimes hear stories of others who ask for direction while in Adoration. Of the many I've heard, one stands out. A lady, feeling very "down," upon entering the Adoration chapel noticed someone lying prostrate on the floor. Inspired by this example of worship, she was able to get outside of herself; her negative feelings vanished, and she felt free to worship Jesus in the monstrance more fully.

A man who often visited the Blessed Sacrament in the chapel also shared a vision he experienced. At the time, he was struggling over whether to make a commitment to marry. While in Adoration, in his mind's eye, he saw the candle flame followed by a long narrow white road. He questioned if it was a "leading" from Jesus but wasn't certain about the road. The man continued to pray and discern, and after receiving peace, he married.

Childhood memories in need of healing are often resolved in Adoration. Someone I know once related to me that she was praying the Divine Mercy Chaplet in intercession for the Lord's mercy for lukewarm believers. After some period of quiet, she felt the Lord confronting her with her own lukewarm attitude. He showed her how this attitude had originated from a childhood trauma of "fitting in," to be liked. As she journaled this experience, she now clearly realized that she needed healing, which enabled her to then move into another ministry.

It is amazing how profound intimacy with Jesus can occur in one holy hour. Yet, equally we can miss the opportunity for intimacy and healing by cutting short our time in Adoration. We might come late or leave early or be too legalistic with our time in front of the Blessed Sacrament.

Although each moment of adoring the Lord is holy, we can lose out on graces that flow if we don't give ourselves enough time. Linda Schubert offers these beautiful, encouraging words about Eucharistic Adoration. In *Miracle Hour,* she says:

I encourage you to come to prayer with an attitude of

openness and expectancy. Come remembering all the ways God has helped you in the past, and come expecting him to help you even more in the future. Consider the "Miracle Hour" as an intensely loving "power encounter" with your heavenly Father. It's a time of cleansing, deeper consecration and growth in understanding of the ways of God. Come accepting and expecting his love. Come prepared to experience his goodness and mercy. Come with a yielded heart that says simply, 'Lord, change me.' Come to be transformed, loosened up, healed and empowered.[6]

Jesus instructed his disciples before his passion in Matthew 26:38-40:

> Then he said to them, "My soul is sorrowful, even to death. Remain here and keep watch with me." . . . . When he returned to his disciples he found them asleep. He said to Peter, "So you could not keep watch with me *one hour*?"

And Jesus went away for the second time and prayed. Matthew 26:43-45:

> Then he returned once more and found them asleep, for they could not keep their eyes open. He left them and withdrew again and prayed a third time, saying the same

thing again. Then he returned to his disciples and said to them, "Are you still sleeping and taking your rest? . . ."

† † †

In *Consoling the Heart of Jesus,* Fr. Michael Gaitley writes of what Jesus needs from us. He wrote that when Jesus appeared to Blessed Margaret Mary in front of the exposed Blessed Sacrament that he spoke of how much he loved mankind and how much he had given for those who had no gratitude and were indifferent.

Fr. Gaitley wrote that Jesus has one desire, and that desire has been described as "thirst." Jesus wants all mankind to love him, but because there is so little love, he is a man of sorrows. He wants all humanity to come into his communion of love with the Father and the Holy Spirit (John 17:24).

Fr. Gaitley asks us to imagine that Jesus says to us: "Behold this heart which loves so much, *yet is so little loved.* Is there anyone who will console this Heart? Is there anyone who will be my friend?"[7]

How significant is this question that Jesus asks of us! He wants a friendship with us. In John 15:14-16, we read how Jesus called his disciples his friends for he made known to them all that the Father said to him. Jesus chose them and appointed them.

Jesus chooses us also to be his friends. "Draw Me Close

to You" is a worship song that is meaningful. The lyrics continue, "Never let me go. I'd lay it all down again—to hear you say that you're my friend. You are my desire, no one else will do."

Will we say "yes" to be his friend?

We are so privileged to have opportunities—daily, if we wish—to be his friend in the reception of Holy Eucharist or in private Adoration in a holy hour. Yet, what stops us? Why is daily Mass not "standing room only" or church holy hours or private Adoration chapels not "full to overflowing"?

First, do we not realize that Jesus "thirsts" for our attention, our love? Secondly, do we know how to withdraw from our busyness, our activities, our talking, and embrace our fears about being silent? Or, thirdly, do we know how much we need to be face-to-face with Jesus so he can re-fuel us and heal us?

If we are not aware of a spiritual hunger for time with Jesus, perhaps our prayer can be for that "first love" to burn within us again. We can pray to the Holy Spirit to enlighten our minds and hearts. There is an ebb and flow to our relationship with Jesus, and when we notice the "ebb," we might ask, "why" and pray for the invocation of the Holy Spirit:

> Come Holy Spirit, fill the hearts of your faithful and enkindle in them the fire of your love. Lord, send forth your Spirit. And you will renew the face of the earth.

† † †

Once in the sacrament of Reconciliation, I was in much distress in confessing the sin of sloth. Secretly, I was hoping that the priest would say that what I confessed was not sloth, but surprisingly, he agreed. The sin was that I had grown slack in my alone time with God. After I confessed this "ebb," the priest provided the grace that I needed to empty myself and fill up again with new resolve and to come before Jesus in silence.

I do not believe that many Catholics understand that Jesus "thirsts" for our love and reparation for our sins. They haven't made the connection noted by Fr. Gaitley. Jesus is to be happy in heaven, but he is still sorrowful that all men don't recognize his great love, sacrifice, and mercy.

Secondly, there is the shift needed, both externally and internally, to leave a stimulating world on many levels, and shift one's attention to an inner world of quiet and silence where we can truly listen, with God speaking within.

In Luke 10:42, Jesus told Martha, in her anxiety, that Mary had chosen "the better part." Mary, who sat at the Lord's feet and listened to his teaching, had done the "one thing" needed. It is much easier to be a Martha than a Mary, who sits in silence with the Master and lets him teach.

In his book *The Power of Silence: Against the Dictatorship of Noise,* Robert Cardinal Sarah wrote: "God speaks in the silence, and silence alone seems to express him."[8]

He said further:

> "The depth of the human soul is God's house. We will be able to let God act by keeping the most perfect interior silence. And it is possible for us to find this silence by being attentive to the voice of silence. Even in a hostile environment, we can find God in ourselves if we seek to listen to the silence that he impresses on our soul."[9]

Thirdly, do we fear silence because we will be face-to-face with ourselves and with Jesus? If we do not go inward when led and seek his healing of the hurts in our lives, our emotional barriers may impede our knowing the fullness of joy and love in the Lord. Our masks stay on!

One of my favorite scriptures is from Philippians 2:9-11:

> Because of this, God greatly exalted him and bestowed on him the name that is above every name, that at the name of Jesus every knee should bend, of those in heaven and on earth and under the earth, and every tongue confess that Jesus Christ is Lord.

† † †

We will end the chapter with three great saints who bowed before Jesus and proclaimed him Lord in Eucharistic Adoration, as well as in life.

In *Saint John Paul the Great: His Five Loves,* author Jason Evert wrote of how Pope St. John Paul II would kneel before the Blessed Sacrament and pray with petitions, prayers for healing, conversions, and others early in the morning. After going to the sacristy to don his vestments for the Mass, he would then again take time to sit or kneel for another ten or twenty minutes.

To others it appeared that he was always in the midst of prayer, loving the Lord. And Evert wrote that although St. John Paul II loved to pray in the wilderness, his favorite place to pray was before the Blessed Sacrament. He spent hours at a time and sometimes the whole night. This great saint spent time in Adoration before every Wednesday audience and made small visits before and after every meal and before and after his pilgrimages.

St. Teresa of Calcutta was also devoted to Adoration. She and her sisters saw many fruits, which she described this way:

> Every evening, when we return from our work we come together in our chapel for an hour of continuous adoration. In the stillness of the moment of the setting sun, we find peace in the presence of Christ. This hour of

intimacy with Jesus is crucial. I saw a great transformation accomplished in our congregation ever since the day we established the practice of daily adoration. Our love for Jesus has become more familiar, more integrated as part of the family and has increased the love that we have for one another. Our love for the sick has become more compassionate. [10]

The *Catechism of the Catholic Church* offers this quote from St. John Paul II's Dominicae cenae, 3:

The church and the world have a great need for Eucharistic worship. Jesus awaits us in this sacrament of love. Let us not refuse the time to go to meet him in Adoration, in contemplation, full of faith, and open to making amends of the serious offenses and crimes of the world. Let our adoration never ease (*CCC*, 1380).

O come let us adore him! As Psalm 95:6 urges:

Enter, let us bow down in worship; let us kneel before the Lord who made us. For he is our God, we are the people he shepherds, the sheep in his hands.

St. Faustina in her *Diary* received a message from Jesus:

There are souls with whom I can do nothing. They

are souls that are continuously observing others but know nothing of what is going on within their own selves. They talk about others continually, even during times of grand silence, which is reserved for speaking only with Me. Poor souls, they do not hear My words; their interior remains empty. They do not look for me within their own hearts, but in idle talk, where I am never to be found. [11]

So, let us take time to be with Jesus in Eucharistic Adoration and give him our whole hearts. He wants to speak and heal in the silence. He wants you to come as you are and allow him to reveal who you truly are and who you *can* be.

CHAPTER 5

Reconciliation and Prayer

In the Catholic world, I find many people will shy away from the practice of Reconciliation. As a Marriage and Family therapist for most of my professional life, and even as a Spiritual Director, I tend to be in the position of hearing men and women's very personal lives that lean toward a "confessional" of sorts. As the person grows to trust me, more and more of the shame of actions or inactions come to the surface. And I always consider it an honor when people share unreconciled, difficult parts of their lives. As a priest once told us at a spiritual direction cenacle, "This is holy ground."

And it truly is! As a therapist, I could listen non-judgmentally and carefully, with empathy, to each person and bring into his or her awareness the issues and talk about God's love and forgiveness, where appropriate. But what was most useful was to suggest, when appropriate, that the person consider the sacrament of Reconciliation. If the person was not Catholic, I might suggest that the person consult his pastor for a confidential meeting.

In his riveting CD, *Confession*,[1] Fr. Larry Richards confronts this topic, head on, and recounts a particularly telling story from one of his many men's conferences.

While on a tour in Rome, a very sturdy-looking man approached Fr. Larry and asked if he would hear his confession. Since there was no formal confessional, Fr. Larry told him he would hear this man's confession on the spot. But he could tell this big, weight-lifter type was nervous and ashamed. Fr. Larry said, "Relax, let me give you a blessing." So, he blessed the man and then told him, "Go for it."

The man told him he'd had sex with two male prostitutes and had been addicted to phone sex most of his life. Fr. Larry interrupted him and exclaimed: "Do you know how much God loves you?" And then followed, "Jesus Christ died to set you free from sin."

Fr. Larry talked about how we meet Jesus in the confessional. He gave his blood at Calvary and with this blood, he freed us from the chains that bind us. We are forgiven our sins at Baptism and then through ongoing sacramental forgiveness. Fr. Larry said we can commit a 100 billion mortal sins and that there is nothing we can do to stop God from loving us.

"God doesn't change, we do," Fr. Larry said. Isn't it beautiful to think that no matter what we do, as bad as we are, or think we are, God stays right with us and keeps loving us? To hear the example of the 100 billion mortal sins and God still loves us—wow, that feels good.

I don't know about you, but I need to hear story after story about God's love, especially from a priest. I like to experience not only the words, but also the countenance of the priest who practices that loving, non-judgmental attitude—in the confessional especially.

Just like the example of the muscular guy in Rome, we can be so ashamed about our sins, even the slightest ones, that we have trouble loving ourselves. And when we have deep and dark sins, we especially need constant re-assurance of God's love because we cannot imagine God could love—or much less forgive—us in the perceived horror we have done or because of how we might feel about ourselves.

Yet, the priest is God's representative, and thank God we have him! In *St. Faustina's Diary*, she records these words of Jesus:

> When you approach the confessional, know this, that I Myself am waiting there for you. I am only hidden by the priest, but I Myself act in your soul.[2]

And St. John Paul II explains: "In the sacrament of Reconciliation, we are all invited to meet Christ personally." He said it's so vital, as it offers each of us "a more personal encounter with the crucified, forgiving Christ with Christ saying through the minister of the sacrament,… 'Your sins are forgiven; go and do not sin again.'"[3]

In his confessions recording, Fr. Larry said that sin makes us feel dirty. And yet, Jesus wants to meet us in the "dirtiness" of our feelings and our sins—just where we are, in the midst of our sin—and he reconciles us to himself and to the body of Christ.

The *Catechism of the Catholic Church* states:

> Only God forgives sins. Since he is the Son of God, Jesus says of himself, "The Son of man has authority on earth to forgive sins" and exercises this divine power: "Your sins are forgiven." Further, by virtue of his divine authority he gives this power to men to exercise in his name (*CCC*, 1441).

He further gave his disciples the power to forgive sins and the authority to reconcile sinners with the Church. This ecclesial part of the task is seen in Christ's words to Simon Peter:

> "I will give you the keys of the kingdom of heaven, and whatever you bind on earth shall be bound in heaven, and whatever you loose on earth shall be loosed in Heaven." The office of binding and loosing which was given to Peter was also assigned to the college of the apostles united to its head (*CCC*, 1444).

However, as I teach church classes and offer spiritual direction, I meet Catholics who have carried years of sin, steeped in unforgiveness of self, and therefore, they dread Confession. Some have given up the Sacrament altogether, ignoring it as part of their Catholic faith. They don't recognize the grace they can receive, but seem to be stuck, not knowing how to handle the sacrament, and therefore not doing anything. In some cases, they may have experienced a difficult confession, or they may just perceive there is too much sin.

In *Lord Have Mercy*, Dr. Scott Hahn writes of the sacrament of Reconciliation and grace:

> The sacrament has been instituted by Christ to give grace. It is an act of God–this sacramental forgiveness of sins–on a par with the creation of the world. Moreover, unlike our other voluntary penances, the sacrament produces its effects by the power of Christ alone, and not at all by our own labors or the labors of our priest-confessor.[4]

In his book *The 7 Secrets of Confession*, author and musician Vinny Flynn explains that the purpose of every sacrament in the church is to give grace, and "the purpose of grace is to heal and sanctify, then the ultimate goal of each sacrament is to heal us and make us holy so that we can become like God."[5]

Fr. Larry Richards acknowledges that some have had negative experiences with Confession and even tells of his own experience as a boy confessing to a priest who yelled at him and even yelled at little old ladies. He affirms that:

Jesus did not go to the cross to kick you and tell you "You're no good." He went to the cross to set you free from your sin and slavery. He gives you a brand-new life forever.[6]

In classes I teach, or with spiritual directees, I try to open the door for them to speak about Confession experiences which may be positive or negative. This offers them an opportunity to discuss their feelings and receive feedback, and possibly lead to a change of mind and heart.

If they've had a negative experience, they may be willing to take a risk and seek Reconciliation, trusting that God will provide a priest who is understanding, so that the experience will be holy and healthy. Perhaps a bigger step is examining their consciences to see if there might be some resentment or unforgiveness that should be confessed and sharing with the priest about their previous bad experience. They may be surprised on the healing that follows.

Once, I was facilitating for the separated and divorced and cancelled the night's class so we could all attend a retreat offered by a visiting priest. I knew that the priest was offering Reconciliation on this night. One man in my class who had avoided the opportunities for Confession for twelve years decided to try it again. He told me later he had a phenomenal experience; it was the beginning of a new chapter in his love relationship with God.

St. Faustina in hearing from Jesus recorded:

> You make your confession before me. The person of the priest is, for Me, only a screen. Never analyze what sort of priest it is that I am making use of; open your soul in confession as you would to Me, and I will fill it with my light.[7]

So, we must not be concerned about who the priest is, but we must stay with the ultimate value of Reconciliation that Jesus talks about. The man from our class took a big step, as he did not know the priest giving the retreat. After hearing his teaching and compassion in the teaching, he overcame fear and decided to take a chance. I believe the Holy Spirit was leading him; as a result, he "came back" to the Church, refreshed and ready to find God again. He has been eternally grateful for this priest, for his help in creating a renewal of his faith and life, as well as a new outlook on the sacrament of Reconciliation.

I imagine there was untold joy in heaven when this man came back to the Father's love, just like in the story of the Parable of the Lost Son; the younger son had lost everything and separated himself from his father (Luke 15:11-32).

In his book *Freedom and Forgiveness: A Fresh Look at the Sacrament of Reconciliation,*[8] Fr. Paul Farren points out that the younger son knew the *one thing* that he still had was his father. The son knew that he could go back to his father. And then he had to work out what he would say.

Isn't that what we sometimes do when we are ready to make that confession? I know I do. Then the father saw his younger son a long way off and was filled with compassion; *and heard his son's confession.* The father ordered the finest robe, a ring for his finger, and sandals for his feet. He then ordered the fattened calf for a feast and celebration. And he said to the elder brother when he protested, "But now we must celebrate and rejoice, because your brother was dead and has come to life again; he was lost and has been found" (Luke 15:32).

I reflect on this parable often. I have had many positive experiences in the sacrament of Reconciliation, and some stand out today as life changing. Yet even with all the positive, healing experiences, there is still a remnant of fear—even dread—at times, prior to Confession. Often our perception of God, which transfers to the priest, is of a judge with a little black book of wrongdoings, keeping count of all our sins. We may come into the confessional shaking, nervous, ashamed, and perhaps like the younger son in the parable above, expecting to be reprimanded.

Fr. Paul Farren writes:

If our image of God is one of an uncompromising judge, then the sacrament can fill us with dread. This is the God of the Big Book who writes down all our sins and forgets none of them.[9]

We may even conjure up this image of God as "judge" from our family-of-origin. It just so happens that my father was a federal judge. But even before he became a judge, I was used to hearing more about my imperfections than my strengths. I perceived that I had to be perfect to receive my father's love; and although my father probably did not keep a little black book on me, *I did.*

I not only have to battle this harsh and unloving external image that can be transferred to the priest-confessor, I must also let go of my own internal critic.

In the moment of dread or nervousness before seeking Confession, I can identify to some extent with the "lost son" in the parable above. The lost son that is perhaps not truly repentant yet, but desperate, with nothing to eat, without any resources, and has to humble himself, in spite of his great sin, and trust his father to take care of him even though he might not deserve it. He trusts that his father will take him back and returns.

Whether my sins are big or little, I feel desperate with sin and unsure, but I have to trust my Heavenly Father's love and mercy, humbling myself, knowing like the "lost son" that I can go back again and again to a Father who will receive me and love me, in spite of my actions.

Fr. Farren writes of becoming like a little child. He writes further that we may want to grow out of this, but there is still a child in each of us who feels vulnerable and fragile; we need a parent who will love us with unconditional acceptance. He says that to receive the gift of the sacrament, we need to listen and respond like the little child who humbles himself, much like the lost son who comes to his father broken and needing love and forgiveness.

Realizing my remnant image of the judge, I pray that I can allow the little child in me to be vulnerable, and I ask the Good Father to transform this negative image and replace it with an image of truth—God's love that is unconditional, which is calling me to come back to him with all my heart.

† † †

I love the familiar song "Hosea," that we hear most often during the liturgical season of Lent. The lyrics include, "Come back to me with all your heart. Don't let sin keep us apart." This beloved song reminds me that God longs for my heart and wants to be close to me; He longs for *you* in the same way.

The image of God the Father which is most tender for me is that of the Good Shepherd. In the parable of the lost sheep, the Good Shepherd leaves the ninety-nine and goes after the one who is lost. And we are told that when he finds it, he rejoices over it more than over the ninety who did not go astray (Matthew 18:12-14).

Putting myself into the scripture, Ignatian style, [10] and becoming the "lost sheep," I can ask the Lord to give me the experience of being the lost sheep in some form and being rescued by the shepherd who has left the others to find me and bring me back. Meditating on this positive image brings healing from the negative one.

In seeking a clearer understanding of the sacrament of Reconciliation, I discovered many titles and subtitles in the *Catechism of the Catholic Church* which provided a more extensive view of the *depth* of this powerful sacrament.

It is a sacrament of *conversion* because "it makes sacramentally present Jesus' call to conversion." It is called the sacrament of *Penance* because "it consecrates the Christian sinner's personal and ecclesial steps of conversion, penance, and satisfaction."

It is called the sacrament of *Confession* since there is disclosure to the priest, and it is also a confession of the "acknowledgment and praise—of the holiness of God and his mercy toward sinful man." It is called the sacrament of *forgiveness* since by the "priest's sacramental absolution God grants the penitent 'pardon and peace.'" Finally, it is the sacrament of *Reconciliation* because it gives to the penitent the love of God, enabling him to go and be reconciled to his brother (*CCC*, 1423, 1424, 1449, and 1442).

The Church also gives us classifications of sins as mortal or venial sins. This can give us help in forming a right conscience and looking at problem areas of our lives. We have to have a way to look at sin. Sin exists and according to Flynn in his *7 Secrets* book, "Every action either strengthens our relationship with God or weakens it."[11]

Quoting Pope John Paul II, Flynn writes:

> To sin is not merely to deny God. To sin is also to live as if he did not exist, to eliminate him from one's daily life.[12]

In a mortal sin, the action is a very serious violation that is deadly to the soul because it does away with the love that God has placed there and separates the person from Him. In order to define the sin as "mortal," I have to know that the choice I make is opposed to God's law. I have to further, with this knowledge, make a personal and deliberate choice to sin in this way (*CCC*, 1587).

Venial sins, the second classification of sins, "weakens our wills, but does not kill us," says Dr. Scott Hahn.[13] However, he writes that we do better if we discern these sins and consider asking forgiveness in the confessional.

The Glossary of the *Catechism of the Catholic Church* defines venial sins in this way:

Venial sin is the failure to observe necessary moderation, in lesser matters of the moral law, or in grave matters acting without full knowledge or complete consent (*CCC*, 1862).

Most times, I find myself confessing venial sins. I will often question myself: "Is this a sin?" or "Will the priest think I am foolish in confessing this?" As the *Catechism* states, "Deliberate and unrepented venial sin disposes us little by little to commit mortal sin" (*CCC*, 1863). I receive the Eucharist often, and I seek additional grace by bringing my thoughts/feelings/sins to the confessional.

† † †

I remember one time feeling down about my resentful feelings toward someone whom I thought was emotionally neglecting her husband. Aware of the negative stirring in my heart, I confessed the resentment to a priest. I was surprised when, for my penance, he asked me to meditate on how much love the man I thought was being emotionally neglected had for his wife.

I tried this meditation and found that this act enabled me to experience the love on both sides. With this priest's loving and wise approach, an abundance of grace opened for me, so I could forgive the woman, think differently about her, and even love her in a new way.

Another time, I was irritable with my husband—not in words, but in my heart. Confessing this time was very difficult as the priest knows both of us. It made the experience more humiliating, and yet again, as I humbled myself with this confession, I found God's grace through the priest. As I faced the priest and he absolved me of my sin, I felt cleansed and ready for a richer marriage. Had I not gone to confession, those thoughts could have developed into resentment of unforgiveness and resulted in negative actions.

Over the years, several persons have said their priest told them they had a "good confession." It made me wonder, *What is a "good confession?"* Fr. Kevin McQuone, a priest with the Diocese of Pensacola-Tallahassee, once told me, "A good confession is one where the penitent has prayerfully prepared, with the help of the Holy Spirit, to know and renounce one's sins and renew one's trust in God's Divine Mercy that is infinitely greater than one's sins."

Fr. Larry Richards says that to have a good confession one should go at least monthly and that it is "good for the soul." My husband and I have practiced monthly Reconciliation for some time as a vital part of the First Saturday devotion given by Our Lady of Fatima to the three children.

Through a private revelation to Fatima visionary Sister Lucia, the Blessed Mother instructed a devotion that would help her spiritual sons and daughters be faithful doing the heavenly Father's will and loving and serving Jesus.

There are four actions that our Lady asked us to do on five consecutive first Saturdays in order to grow spiritually. We are to go to confession, receive Communion, recite five decades of the rosary, and be with our Blessed Mother for fifteen minutes while meditating on the mysteries of the rosary.

Our Lady does not want us to miss graces when we neglect the sacrament of confession by only going yearly. So, if we go to confession on a regular monthly basis, she says we will always remain in a state of grace.

In *Fatima Today*, Fr. Andrew Apostoli said going monthly "means that God will always live in us."[14] Isn't this a beautiful thought? That God's grace is always with us. I don't know about you, but I need all the grace I can get.

In his description of a "good confession," Fr. Apostoli said an examination of conscience beforehand helps us to look at our relationship with God. With a good confession and absolution by the priest, we are relieved from the oppression that sin can cause, and our souls can receive peace. With the special grace, we can be helped to avoid sin in the future, and we can at that time make a resolution of how to go about our lives differently. We may even decide to practice certain virtues. It is also wonderful to receive the encouragement of the priest-confessor.

Scott Hahn writes that we should make a confession that is "complete and contrite."[15] He suggests making an examination of conscience daily, principally at bedtime, for five to ten minutes and to take notes. Having a mid-day examination also gives you plenty of time for correction in the day.

When lining up or sitting in the room or chapel waiting for my Reconciliation, I humble myself, and hope and pray that I can make a "good confession." I try to give up my pride and become "little" as I enter into the sacrament of Reconciliation. I also pray and ask the Lord, through the power of the Holy Spirit, and in my examination of conscience, to bring to my mind the sins that Jesus wants confessed. I ask Him to move deeply to get to what may be difficult for me to face, but what Jesus wants. For Jesus wants me to be free of anything that will keep me from loving God fully. And I want to be reconciled with the Church.

As I prepare, hopefully, for a "good confession," I ask myself two essential questions from the commandments Jesus emphasized to the scholar of the law (Matthew 22:36-40): "How have I failed to love God with all my heart, my soul, and my mind?" And, "How have I failed to love my neighbor in my thoughts, words, and deeds?" With this examination, I hope to have a confession that brings me into a fuller love relationship with God. And this is where prayer is essential again.

I also like Vinny Flynn's regimen offered in his *7 Secrets* book. He has his list of behaviors that need forgiveness, but he also asks himself where he needs healing in his relationship with God. Where does he not feel at peace? Is he angry,

depressed, anxious, bitter, or resentful? Where is he too focused on himself? What areas of his life has he not given to
Jesus? What areas of his life does he want to keep hidden
from Jesus? These are good "Examen" questions that can
bear much fruit for the subject of confession.

Pope Benedict XVI said the priest is not just there to
grant absolution but is "called to take on the role of father,
spiritual guide, teacher, and educator." [16] And at that moment, these other roles came forward.

Once, my husband and I were watching a movie together
and the main character took the Lord's Name in vain many
times. I didn't know what to do—whether to stay in the
movie theater or leave. What I did instead was prayed and
asked forgiveness at the times the Lord's name was taken in
vain. I knew this was one of the Ten Commandments, and
even though I didn't commit the behavior or the sin, I felt
that I was complicit by being present in the movie. I wasn't
sure it was a sin, but as Fr. Larry Richards said, when you
have sinned it feels dirty, and in this instance, I felt guilty
watching the movie and "dirty" enough to go to the priest.

When I confessed to the priest, I asked for a way to think
about this and what stance I should take in that experience.
The priest was empathetic and suggested escape routes. He
said that certainly I could leave the movie, or I could decide
not to recommend the movie to others. He acted as a spiritual guide, and I noticed that I instantly felt better.

My husband and I decided on those routes: that we

would leave the movie if a character offended the Lord's name more than two times, and we would not recommend the movie to others. Since we view movies often, this guideline has worked well for us. It's amazing in our modern times how many ways God is insulted or affronted in movies and television. And it is even more surprising how many Christians/Catholics do not notice.

Pope St. John Paul's devotion to the sacrament of Reconciliation started before he became pope, and he felt that "priests should freely become a prisoner of the confessional. It is in the confessional that his spiritual fatherhood in the fullest way."

Sometimes, he would spend up to an hour with one penitent. As a cardinal he said: "Sin is always a suffering of the human conscience. That is why it is important that, at the moment of confessing our sins, there is on the other side of the confessional screen a man who is sensitive, who can sympathize." [17]

† † †

It's well known that if we continue to commit venial sins, especially the same ones, this can lead to mortal sins.

I recall one time when I failed to confess the sin of lying (I rationalized that this was a "white" lie and done because I did not want to hurt someone's feelings). Unfortunately, I committed a second lie shortly afterward and a priest helped me later to understand that by not confessing, it happened again. Acting as a spiritual guide, the priest recommended an enlightening book: C.S. Lewis, "The Problem of Pain," so that I could understand how sin was a result of woundedness in a person.

After that experience, I was convinced of the necessity of confession *soon* after the sin. All of this led me to wonder, 'Where did this notion of a 'white lie' come from and the idea that it truly didn't matter?' Fortunately, no mortal sins were committed as I was able to get that sin out of the way with the priest.

As we continue to work for God in his church, it is important to be reconciled with him, and that our relation-ship of love with him is restored through the forgiveness of our sins offered through Reconciliation. We are "freer," and the obstacles are removed so that we can bring God's love to others.

† † †

Recently a group of us assisted a priest during a healing service that had over seven hundred people in attendance. Our role was to console anyone he designated who might be crying or who needed extra attention which he could not give in the ministering and anointing of such a vast crowd.

Fortunately, I had learned from the example of many mentors in healing ministries that it's important to seek Reconciliation prior to ministry. After I received absolution from my sins, the priest affirmed the decision, saying that if I had any unresolved area or unforgiveness, it might trigger me, or somehow interfere when I'm working with someone.

St. John Vianney is considered the patron of parish priests. Although he had difficulty with his formal education for the priesthood, he had a vision for his life's work. In addition to opening a school for girls in France, his main focus was on the confessional. His dedication to the priesthood was shown when in the winter months he spent eleven to twelve hours daily hearing people's confessions. And in the summer, he increased it to sixteen hours.

It is written that Fr. Padre Pio also spent most of his day hearing confessions. From 1918 to 1923, he heard confessions fifteen to nineteen hours a day. It is said that 83,035 women and 19,837 men registered for confession in 1962. And in 1970, he averaged 70 people per day. People came to him from around the world.

Jesus once told St. Faustina, "When you go to confession . . . the Blood and Water which came forth from My Heart always flows down upon your soul and ennobles it. [18]

I recall Scott Hahn's encouraging words in *Lord Have Mercy* to take time to get to Reconciliation often. He encourages all to make a confession every week or every month, rather than once a year. It gets easier, he said, just like a tennis game becomes "smoother with practice."[19]

Because I'm a tennis player, I can relate to that analogy. If I stay away from a tennis game too long, I find that my forehand stroke and my backhand stroke will suffer, as will my serve. Once I arrive at the center, I find that the "tennis fever" hits me, and I am racing to get to the court. Going to Reconciliation at least monthly, I am not so rusty. I can remember my faults, first of all, and that is a feat for me. And, secondly, I get into the pattern of knowing where I need the extra grace that I know the sacrament offers.

Like tennis fever, believe it or not, I can race to get to the confessional. And that is an accomplishment!

CHAPTER 6

Meditative Prayer

About a year ago I had to admit something to myself: My practice of one of the most important elements in our third order Discalced Carmelite "Rule of Life"—mental prayer — had gone by the wayside.

It had happened gradually. My early morning mental prayer, meditation, and contemplation with God—a practice recommended by St. Alphonsus—had slipped to early afternoon, and then to late afternoon. You can guess what happened next.

On most days, by late afternoon, I was scrambling to get in—or better yet *fit in*—my time with the Lord. I would eventually run out of time, due to a scheduled activity, and lost the window of opportunity to be quiet and intimate with God. It became more and more of a struggle to find the solitude. I was becoming more of a Martha than a Mary.

The example comes to us in Luke 10:41-42:

> The Lord said to her in reply, "Martha, Martha, you are anxious and worried about many things. There is need of only one thing. Mary has chosen the better part and it will not be taken from her."

One day I decided that being a Martha without the Mary wasn't working for me; I had grown more and more frustrated—even despairing. What was I to do? I had too many activities, there was too much distraction, and I ended up without the holy time of mental prayer with God that I so desired and that I know He desired with me.

I was "missing" God! Where was "the better part" referred to in scripture? The idea of "missing God," in some ways, didn't make sense at first. That's because my primary defense mechanism of *rationalization* had kicked in, and I knew it well. The *rationalization* helped me avoid anxiety. My "defense" was that taking more time with spiritual activities and other forms of prayer was somehow an ade-quate substitute for the quiet, meditative, and contemplative prayer time.

I justified the lapse, asking myself: Wasn't I with God during the spiritual writing, thinking about him, looking up scripture, praying through some paragraphs? Wasn't I with God at Mass and when I was interceding for others in praying the rosary, the Divine Mercy Chaplet, and novena and various other prayers?

What was the problem? After all, I was seeking God.

What saved me for awhile was my two hours weekly in Adoration at two local churches. While these were lifesavers for my mental prayer, again, it still wasn't enough. What had come to a standstill was the consistent practice of *daily* mental prayer and the contemplative life in my home. Sometimes it happened, sometimes not.

In my continued desperation, I remembered the fourteen rules of discernment from St. Ignatius of Loyola[1]. I'd read about them in the prologue to Fr. Tim Gallagher's book *The Discernment of Spirits: An Ignatian Guide for Everyday Living*. St. Ignatius described reflecting when his "eyes were opened a little." And that is what I did. As I reflected on my dilemma, and "my eyes were opened just a little," I realized that I was in desolation either psychological or spiritual or both.

I knew that I had to follow the Ignatian guidelines to get back on track. After much examination (Rule no. 6), the Holy Spirit was directing me to acknowledge my negligence before God, to repent, and get to Reconciliation to set straight my pathway to God and my life as a Carmelite.

In a person moving forward in the relationship with God (Rule no. 2), St. Ignatius warned that the evil one would attempt to weaken the movement toward God with disquiet and agitation, with that person becoming slothful and tepid, feeling as if separated from God. In my case, there was the temptation to omit my prior practices in my prayer life, which led me away from God with the above elements of sloth, tepidity, and separation taking hold.

I finally decided it was high time I admitted this neglect of mine to a priest in confession. I needed grace!

As I sat in the Marian chapel of the church waiting for the confessional to open and reviewing my sin, I literally shook in my boots. I questioned myself and thought: "How could I confess such a sin to the priest?" Since I am a professed member of the Discalced Carmelites, this seemed like one of the worst venial sins[2], given that it was part of my Rule of Life. It felt more like a grave sin.

And yet again, the Holy Spirit reminded me, that no matter what the sin(s), Reconciliation is about receiving the sacramental grace needed, and I knew that as humiliated as I felt about admitting the sin, the need for grace overcame the embarrassment and fear of the whole thing.

Once in the confessional, I managed to overcome my discomfort and acknowledge my position as a Discalced Carmelite to give the priest an understanding of how terrible the sin was to me. I wondered if he even needed that preface, but I gave it anyway. As I spoke, I noticed I held his gaze, and he was even nodding his head in recognition. I thought to myself, either he has confessed this sin himself, or he has heard this sin before. But I dared not ask!

Thankfully, being honest with the priest, receiving absolution for my sin, and realizing that God still loved me worked, and I was able to reconvene that time with Jesus in the mornings. Now, I am careful to safeguard that quiet time—"the better part." And I remain alert to how my secular world, plus the evil one, can get me out of my spiritual routine.

† † †

I call the type of prayer I'm referencing "mental prayer." In the earlier scripture, Jesus tells Martha that Mary has "chosen the better part and it shall not be taken away from her." In his book, *Prayer Primer,*[3] Fr. Thomas Dubay writes that many assume prayer means "vocal" prayer only, and he further comments that it is rare to hear a homily on meditation or contemplation. As I think back over the years, I am not aware of one homily in which this subject was addressed.

So how is mental prayer defined? Mental prayer is often divided into meditation and contemplation. Sometimes, we hear them spoken of as one process. I think this occurs because they are part of the same process, *meditation* often leading to contemplation and both leading to intimacy with God.

In this chapter, the focus is on *meditation,* followed by contemplation in the next chapter.

In the *Catechism of the Catholic Church,* we learn that "meditation engages thought, imagination, emotion, and desire" (*CCC,* 2708). It is intended to deepen our faith convictions and convert our hearts and strengthen our will to follow Christ.

In another of Fr. Thomas Dubay's books, *Fire Within,* he provides a much detailed discussion of *meditative* prayer through stories about St. Teresa of Jesus (Avila) and St. John of the Cross—both masters in prayer. St. Teresa of Jesus (Avila) encouraged her nuns to turn their inner eyes on Jesus and all aspects of his life as a way to begin their *meditative* prayer. Her favorite *meditation* was on the passion and death of Jesus. She said that meditating on him would fill their souls.[4]

In his book *Fulfillment of All Desire,*[5] Dr. Ralph Martin told of how St. Teresa of Jesus (Avila)'s nuns had an hour of meditation and prayer in the morning and another hour before the evening meal.

For many years now, my spiritual journey has focused on my commitment as a member of the third order (secular) Discalced Carmelite tradition. My "Rule of Life"[6] under the Rule of St. Albert, Patriarch of Jerusalem, includes: Liturgy of the Hours in the morning and evening, frequent Mass, celebration especially of Mass for Marian feast days, spiritual reading, and at least thirty minutes daily of *mental prayer*, which includes *meditation* and contemplation.

I find the following words a beautiful expression of the Carmelite experience. In the introduction to *The Spirituality of St. Teresa of Avila*, Sr. Mary Alphonsetta Haneman, CSSF, writes:

In the spirit of St. Teresa and St. John of the Cross, tertiaries are to be mindful of the presence of the Blessed Trinity in their persons. CARMEL means an enclosed or secret garden in which God himself actually lives and dwells.[7]

And:

> The object of the Third Order is to make each tertiary conscious of the divine indwelling and to come as close as possible to Him in this mortal life.[8]

I think these two quotations express well the intent of *mental prayer*–to find that *secret garden inside* where God dwells. To get there is not easy and requires daily commitment, as I realized after my lapse.

Dan Burke, in *Into the Deep*, reminds us from St. John's description of Jesus that "he first loved us" (1 John 4:19). He goes on to quote the *Catechism of the Catholic Church* which says that God desires to meet us in prayer.

> The wonder of prayer is revealed beside the well where we come seeking water: There, Christ comes to meet every human being. It is he who first seeks us and asks us for a drink. Jesus thirsts; his asking arises from the depths of God's desire for us. Whether we realize it or not, prayer is the encounter of God's thirst with ours. God thirsts that we may thirst for him. (*CCC*, 2560)

It is not that vocal prayers are not good, or that they are unimportant. To put this in perspective, vocal prayers begin our communing with God. Author Ralph Martin in *Fulfill-ment of All Desire* writes that in the time of St. Teresa of Jesus (Avila) and St. Francis de Sales, there was great discussion of vocal and mental prayer. He wrote:

> Vocal prayer—prayer said out loud—was usually un-derstood to be a matter of reciting the memorized pray-ers such as the "Our Father" or the "Hail Mary." Mental prayer was generally understood to be the prayer that was said with the attention of the mind, the words formed interiorly and not spoken out loud.[9]

In *Prayer Primer,* Fr. Thomas Dubay reminds us that Je-sus taught us to address God in human terms in conversa-tion. He taught us, "Ask and you shall receive" and the Lord's prayer.[10] We need to express our feelings and thoughts to God in prayer. It is a natural process, and particularly when we are in distress or pain. It can be a short, 'Jesus help me,' or a longer prayer of the heart that enumerates all sorts of difficulties and petitions for assistance and healing.

However, we can get in trouble by multiplying our vocal prayers and thereby neglecting the "sitting at the feet of Je-sus," as Mary in the scripture above. Or as St. Teresa of Jesus (Avila) commented: "The important thing is not to think much, but to love much."[11]

In his book *Soul of the Apostolate,* Jean-Baptiste Chautard, O.C.D.S., writes of the danger of an apostolic life *without an interior life*. He said that the evil one may speak into the ear of the devout and busy man, who can't seem to get everything done. He will advise him that he is spending too much time in the office, Mass, or doing ministry work and that he needs to cut something out. Perhaps the man shortens his *meditation* time.

St. Alphonsus writes:

> Now for a man in the active life to give up his *meditation* is tantamount to throwing down his arms at the feet of the enemy.
>
> Short of a miracle, a man who does not practice mental prayer will end up in mortal sin. [12]

St. Vincent de Paul tells us:

> A man without mental prayer is not good for anything; he cannot renounce the slightest thing. It is merely the life of an animal. [13]

Further, some authors quote St. Teresa of Jesus (Avila) as having written:

> Without mental prayer a person soon becomes either a brute or a devil. If you do not practice mental prayer, you do not really need any devil to throw you into hell,

you throw yourself in there of your own accord. On the contrary, give me the greatest of all sinners; if he practices mental prayer, be it only for fifteen minutes every day, he will be converted. If he perseveres in it, his eternal salvation will be assured. [14]

These writings by great saints are truly scary; and I feel distressed about those who do not understand the importance or the practice *mental prayer.* At times, those whom I teach in classes, see in spiritual direction, or listen to in counseling need help in *mental prayer, meditative prayer,* in "sitting" with and loving the Lord.

They perform vocal prayers and spiritual activities well, but don't know how to allow the quiet, meditative time with the Lord. Some find it too difficult to sit still, while others express frustration because they fall asleep fighting too many distractions to 'stay the course,' so they stop—just as I did, for a time.

St. Teresa of Jesus (Avila) acknowledges how difficult it is to concentrate. She wrote: "I spent 14 years never being able to practice meditation without reading." [15]

Fr. Dubay in *Fire Within,* discusses meditative prayer for beginners, noting what John of the Cross said about the practice:

… through the delight it affords it draws the beginner away from "sensual things" and the world thus loses some of its appeal. Incipient progress occurs. We are, says John, to see creation and *meditation* only as means to an end and to use them as such. [16]

He continues to explain that we should go with what God gives in his favor, as God will "take us" beyond the meditative into the mystical, described in the next chapter on contemplative prayer.

We start, as beginners, and even beyond, with meditative prayer, as an expression of prayer explained in the *Catechism of the Catholic Church* where a meeting or an encounter with the Lord takes place (*CCC*, 2705-2708).

In beginning mental prayer, St. Teresa wrote that to "go inward" is the first step, gathering the mind and the heart to hear God. She reminds us that a sufficient time needs to be allotted to prayer, so that one can withdraw from the busyness of the world. There is a recollection of oneself, defined as "acquired recollection." I'll speak to this more in the next chapter.

In his book *Signs of Life*, Dr. Scott Hahn suggests we sit in front of the Tabernacle in the church before or after Mass or at other times of the day, advising that it is the best place for optimum quiet, where Jesus can be reverenced.

Dan Burke, author of *Into the Deep*, suggests that we create a place that is dedicated to prayer and nothing else. He writes that you might think that this is impossible to find space to withdraw, yet only a few feet of space is necessary—

even a closet will do.

He recounts a person who crawled into the closet under her clothes and prayed sitting on pillows. He also remarked that his own first prayer space was a combination of a windowsill, an icon, candle, and a small bench. Any place can be suitable, and he recommends icons, candles, or holy images to be present.

Because of my difficulty concentrating, my first prayer experiences in my home occurred in my walk-in closet. I sat on the floor with my big pillow, bible, and journal close at hand. It was quiet—no distractions, no windows, and concentration was "at a peak." My friends laughed at me, saying that I was "closeted," but the Holy Spirit sure worked there!

No more closets in recent years, but I do have a prayer corner in my home. My concentration is optimal here, as a sacred space, only secondary to time in front of the tabernacle. My home prayer space is filled with windows, much light, bibles, spiritual books, numerous pictures of Jesus, Mary, Padre Pio, St Joseph, and some icons. For instance, I have a framed dried flower from the garden of St. Therese, my favorite Carmelite saint; I can reflect and be inspired from her childlike and beautiful, unswerving love for God.

Author Dan Burke also wrote that it is important to remove anything from your space that might draw your attention away–like computers, phones, TVs, as well as other distractions. Meanwhile, the presence of icons and visual aids for mediation, mentioned earlier, helps us be more focused in our prayer.

According to the *Catechism of the Catholic Church*, meditation can be helped by books, the Sacred Scriptures, holy icons, liturgical texts of the day or season, writings of the spiritual fathers, and other words of spirituality (*CCC*, 2705).

Acknowledging the schedules of people who work and have families, St. Francis de Sales recommended setting aside an hour every day before the mid-day meal, suggesting early in the morning when the mind might be less distracted and renewed after the night's rest. He suggested not praying more than an hour, unless directed by one's spiritual director. [17]

† † †

Sometimes, reciting the Jesus prayer ("Lord Jesus Christ, Son of God, have mercy on me, a sinner"), receiving Eucharist, or taking a scene from the Lord's life will help us to be drawn into his presence and out of the exterior world. Also reading the Mass scriptures and meditating on them simply or using a *Lectio Divina* may be enough.

The Catechism of the Catholic Church states that: "Christian prayer tries above all to meditate on the mysteries of Christ, as in Lectio Divina or the rosary" (*CCC*, 2708). I find *Lectio Divina* useful, and, when the opportunity is offered in the church, I teach it.

In his letter to the universal church at the end of the Jubilee year in 2000, St. John Paul II called for all to practice this method of prayer:

> It is especially necessary that listening to the Word of God should become a life-giving encounter, in the ancient and ever valid tradition of *lectio divina*, which draws from the biblical text the living word which questions, directs and shapes our lives.[18]

In his book *Conversing with God: Praying the Sunday Mass Readings with Lectio Divina*, author Stephen Binz describes the practice of *Lectio Divina* as a method of praying with the scriptures to understand how the Lord wants to use the ancient biblical text to speak to us today–in our current situation—and it is powerful.

Lectio divina follows in a "movement" progression, first reading and understanding the sacred text with footnotes or commentaries. Then one meditates on the meaning of the text, asking questions of the text to see how the Holy Spirit is leading. Following this movement is praying in response to the individual meaning in order to see how God desires to use the scripture for revelation. Finally, one rests in the message received through a contemplative approach.

Binz reported that St. Benedict recommended *Lectio Divina* for his monks, especially during Lent, as a way to encounter God. This was 'set in place' to see where they were falling short and determine what more was needed in their personal discipleship. Referencing the scripture and after some sacred reading and then meditation, expecting that the Lord would speak and that the person praying would respond in dialogue to God. Through this practice, a relationship between the ancient text and the personal message the Lord wanted to send was established.

In a beautiful, instructive, and inspiring article by Dr. Tim Gray "Lectio Divina—Stairway to Heaven,"[19] he shows through the work of a Carthusian monk named Guigo how *Lectio Divina,* in the four-step process, mirrors the story of Jacob found in Genesis 28:11-12. In Jacob's dream, he saw the ladder reaching to heaven and angels ascending and descending. When he awoke, he was sure the Lord was there, and he named the place Bethel, which means "House of God" in Hebrew.

Guigo showed further how the fourfold method of *Lectio Divina* are like the four rungs of a ladder; if one kept ascending one step at a time, the soul would get to heaven. The steps would be lectio (reading of the scripture), meditatio (meditation) to seek the truth of what God wants to say to the person, oratio (dialogue) when one can express to God what touches the heart; and finally these rungs can move the person to the gift of contemplatio (contemplation), where there is peace and joy with God.

Contemplation, as described by Guigo, is:

...a pure gift in which our hearts are taken up in a loving gaze of God, as the *final* step. We often come to prayer looking for contemplation, but we begin without the divine dialogue that leads to contemplation. [20]

Guigo explains further that we may try to get to contemplation too quickly and miss the first and second rungs of the ladder that help us in our ascent on the steps. Contemplation is a later stage of prayer, he said. I have discovered this to be the case.

In teaching classes on *Lectio Divina* now for several years, my experience has been that most people especially welcomed the experiential exercises. "Quieting down" and practicing the five-step process for thirty minutes or so provided a start to read, study, and meet God personally in the scripture text. Although this was not the most adequate time, it helped; the "hands on" provided a preparation session. This part of the program made the practice of *Lectio Divina* easier to continue at home.

Participants have said they enjoyed it and were surprised at how the Lord spoke to them in the quiet. Many found the process exciting—opening up a whole new world of experiencing a personal closeness to God in his Word. We offered more than one session, so that there was opportunity for another "rehearsal" of sorts to "practice" for home.

Being with God, reading, and understanding scripture, and then asking questions of God about their own lives was new to many. A few persons, recalling childhood memories, prompted by the scripture passages, found starting points of healing needed.

Others received clarity about a current situation. As I learned about these little miracles taking place, I was amazed again at the power on meditating on God's Word. It was an unqualified delight for me to see that others could be brought into the presence of God so intensely during a simple, time-limited class. Viewing God's work in this process increased motivation and hope for continuing to offer classes.

Dr. Tim Gray writes that some may think that *Lectio Divina* is only for monks; however, it is for everyone. This was made clear by Pope Benedict XVI. On September 16, 2005, he encouraged that everyone use *Lectio Divina*. On the fortieth anniversary of *Dei Verbum,* the Second Vatican Council's great document on Scripture, reads, "If (*Lectio Divina*) is effectively promoted, this practice will bring to the church—I am convinced—a new spiritual springtime."[21]

What a strong statement from Pope Benedict on the value on meditating on scripture. *Lectio Divina,* in my opinion, not only provides healing through scripture, but also opens an internal door to a readiness for contemplation, the subject of our next chapter.

CHAPTER 7

Contemplative Prayer

Do you have a best friend? Think for a moment of who that might be.

When I stop to think about my best friend, I am amazed that I met this person forty years ago and I still call her "best." What a gift she has been to me all these years! What I love most is that she is kind, loving, and spiritually as well as psychologically solid. She's beautiful, intelligent, creative, and more.

She sounds perfect, doesn't she? Well, maybe she is—for in God's eyes, we are all perfect. Perhaps another reason that I call her my "best" friend is that she is unconditionally caring and loves me for who I am—the good, the bad, and the ugly.

In our forty-year friendship, she has seen and heard it all. She is available to chat about the silliest things or to share a difficulty. Our time together can be "chatty," or silent, as we experience a spiritual time together. It makes no difference because the bond of mutual trust and caring is there and never changes. It is ongoing, no matter what the physical distance or time apart.

And that is the way that it can be with Jesus—we can

share a relationship of mutual trust and caring, a bond that never ends. Many of us talk to Jesus throughout the day, and this is how we share time with good friends.

Jesus invites us to a friendship in which we don't even need words. We can sit in silence with him. We can set the stage to experience quiet within by meditating on scripture, spiritual icons, or other elements of the spiritual life, as we saw in the last chapter. We yearn to be with him, content in the silence. And that silence creates a space and inclination for the beginning of contemplative prayer.

So, what is contemplative prayer? And how do we get there? For the moment, let me give a couple of quick answers. Contemplative prayer is a mystical gift and it's God-given; there's a spiritual process that leads to a readiness, so that God can grant the gift.

The *Catechism of the Catholic Church* quotes St. Teresa of Jesus (Avila), who described it this way: "Contemplative prayer in my opinion is nothing else than a close sharing between friends; it means taking time frequently to be alone with him who we know loves us" *CCC*, 2709).

For most of us, sitting and being in the quiet, taking time to be alone with God and allowing God to talk *in* us and talk *to* us, is difficult. You may be wondering what I mean by talking "in" us. Since God is Creator of each of us, he has a unique way of letting us know that he is present. We know his voice and—even in the silence—it is somehow audible to us. It is in this close sharing with him that we have an opportunity to experience his gift of contemplative prayer.

In *Fulfillment of All Desire,*[1] Ralph Martin writes that few people claim to be "contemplative" because they don't know what it means. A "contemplative" is considered someone who has had phenomenal experiences and is associated with cloistered nuns and monks or canonized saints. He asserts further that the term "contemplative" may even seem too lofty for the rest of us.

In his book *Fire Within,*[2] Fr. Thomas Dubay writes that many people think of the term *contemplation* as "frightening or mysterious or esoteric, or possibly all three." He added, "They equate it with oriental states of consciousness or with extraordinary phenomena such as divine message and visions." However, oriental mysticism are states of impersonal awareness, and *contemplation* is an awareness of God's love. "Unlike oriental states of awareness, our prayer is a love communion that the divine beloved himself gives when we are ready for it." And he further clarifies, "Christic contemplation is nothing less than a deep love communion with the triune God."[3]

In a later book by Fr. Dubay, *Prayer Primer: Igniting the Fire Within*, the author points out that in Psalm 1:1-2, the psalter states that the faithful are blessed as they ponder the word of the Lord day and night. "This is the language of advancing contemplative prayer. And these words express the Church's mind, and that of the saints in all states of life, in

saying that meditation and contemplation are for everyone."[4]

† † †

In the last chapter, we spoke of Martha and Mary in the
Gospel of Luke. Let's reflect more deeply on the story, particularly pondering the words that Jesus said about Mary.
You may recall that Mary sat at the feet of Jesus, and Martha
did much serving, but complained and this is the dialogue:

> Martha, burdened with much serving, came to him
> and said, "Lord, do you not care that my sister has left
> me by myself to do the serving? Tell her to help me."
> The Lord said to her in reply, "Martha, Martha, you
> are anxious and worried about many things. There is
> need of only one thing. Mary has chosen the better part
> and it will not be taken from her" (Luke 10:40-42).

The commentary from the *Ignatius Catholic Study Bible*
offers this helpful explanation of that particular scripture:

> ...the two women signify two dimensions of the
> spiritual life. Martha signifies the active life as she busily
> labors to honor Christ through her work. Mary exempli-
> fies the contemplative life as she sits attentively to listen
> and learn from Christ. While both activities are essential

to Christian living, the latter is greater than the former. For in Heaven, the active life terminates, while the contemplative life reaches perfection.[5]

For instance, he created me to be a person who is a "doer" of many spiritual things, more like a Martha, and yet, there is a Mary inside, perhaps less dominant. He does not condemn the "Martha" side, rather, helps me embrace it, use it for his glory, and then move me into the "Mary" side. This is the "better part." For some who have a dominant "Mary" side, there is an opposite process. In his leading, I am moved into the "better part," the depth of my inner being.

I don't hear much instruction about the "better part." We are taught to talk to God and recite many prayers, instead, often leaving the other out. Many spiritual directees, or those whom I counsel, do not realize that there is more and may not seek to find that "better part"—a more contemplative approach, sitting quietly at the feet of Jesus.

Fr. Robert Spitzer, S.J., in *Five Pillars of the Spiritual Life: A Practical Guide to Prayer for the Active People* writes about *contemplation* as the fifth pillar following the Eucharist, spontaneous prayer, the Beatitudes and partnership with the Holy Spirit. The fourth pillar also includes parts of Ignatian spirituality: peace, inspiration, transformation, consolation, desolation, and spiritual discernment.

Fr. Spitzer writes of contemplation as different from spontaneous prayers of petitioning for something specific, for contemplation does not seek relief, forgiveness, inspiration or other, but seeks just to know God more deeply. He writes: "It seeks to know the heart of God, that is, to appreciate God in and for himself."[6] It takes time, silence, and separation from the busyness of life for God to lead you into his heart. Fr. Spitzer says that often we don't give ourselves enough space to "see how lovely contemplation on God's love can be."[7] He suggests going on retreat to discover it.

I agree that retreats are wonderful and will provide us with the space and silence, if we're willing, to be led further into the depths of God. Scott Hahn in his book *Signs of Life* writes that all of us should "make" a retreat annually. However, we don't always have access to a retreat, or may not be able to get there when God calls us to "the more." When we hear his call, just as the fisherman did so long ago, we must "drop our nets" and eagerly follow his path leading within us, wherever we are in our day-to-day walk.

For, as Fr. Spitzer rightly pointed out, to move into contemplative prayer we must give our time and silence and wait for God to lead us into his heart, something we don't often do. He further suggests that we "don't give ourselves enough space."[8]

Fr. Spitzer mentions that often one will begin prayer time with rote prayers, meditation, or both, and then find that the love relationship with God will become deeper and more rooted as we separate from the busyness of life.

Separating from the busyness of life is difficult for most of us. Often people speak of how busy they are and the challenge of finding the quiet. In a recent workshop, I heard a very respected and devout man say that he could not quiet himself to pray. He talked about his active missionary work and the good that, indeed, he did. Yet, staying active in the service of God with many works, but without the benefit of silence with God, may rob the person of that very personal, intimate contemplative relationship—that gift from the Lord.

The *Catechism of the Catholic Church* acknowledges meditation as an expression of prayer and is of great value, then continues: "…but Christian prayer should go further: to the knowledge of the love of the Lord Jesus, to union with him" (*CCC*, 2708).

The idea of presence is central to prayer, an "awareness that God is within, up close and personal," insists Discalced Carmelite friar Fr. Eugene McCaffrey. In his book *Let Nothing Trouble You: Teresa The Woman, The Guide, and the Storyteller,*[9] he writes, "It is not a question of words but of silence, attentiveness and listening." He tells how St. Teresa of Jesus (Avila) recommended simply that one talk to God with "no need for long meditation or reflection; you have only to look at him with the eyes of the soul." Truly, "rest in his presence."

Fr. McCaffrey explains further that St. Teresa wants us to know that God is within and wants us to be there with him.

In her image of the "interior castle," she writes of a dwelling place of "priceless beauty." She said, "We need no wings to go in search of it: all we have to do is to look within, with eyes of love, and open our hearts to the call of the Beloved."

The *Catechism of the Catholic Church* explains the concept further:

> Entering into contemplative prayer is like entering into Eucharistic liturgy; we "gather up" the heart, recollect our whole being under the prompting of the Holy Spirit, abide in the dwelling place of the Lord which we are, awaken our faith in order to enter into the presence of him who awaits us. We let our masks fall and turn our hearts back to the Lord who loves us, so as to hand ourselves over to him as an offering to be purified and transformed (*CCC*, 2711).

Knowledge of the love of God and "union" with him is described well by St. Teresa of Jesus (Avila) in her book *The Interior Castle*, which highlights prayer through seven dwelling places or mansions of the soul, in which the seventh dwelling place is union.

The Church considers St. Teresa as well as St. John of the Cross experts on contemplative life. And both saints have been declared doctors of the universal Church, and, as Fr. Dubay's book *Fire Within* states, they have much to say about contemplative prayer and the way to get to it.

They present the Church's mind about mystical prayer and about the deep things of God. Seeking "union" with God, or permitting him to take us there, is deep. "Union" may seem like an impossibility through prayer, but our Carmelite saints, particularly St. Teresa of Jesus (Avila) and St. John of the Cross, have shown us it can be accomplished.

God loves us and wants us to know him *within*, and the *Catechism of the Catholic Church* states that contemplation is a gift from God:

> Contemplative prayer is the simplest expression of the mystery of prayer. It is a *gift*, a grace; it can be accepted only in humility and poverty. Contemplative prayer is a covenant relationship established by God within our hearts. Contemplative prayer is a communion in which the Holy Trinity conforms man, the image of God, "to his likeness" (*CCC*, 2713).

† † †

St. John of the Cross had many gifts; and Fr. Dubay stated that his "greatest talent was his poetic genius."[10] He said although he was absorbed in God and also experienced ecstatic prayer, the great saint wrote little about the subject since it was so well covered in the writings of his friend, St. Teresa of (Jesus) Avila.

In his writings about contemplative prayer, however, St. John of the Cross made a delineation through exploring the dark night of the senses and the dark night of the spirit, which are invaluable to grasp the totality of the contemplative experience as well as clear up some confusion. He, like St. Teresa, reached transforming union with God. And the fruit of his contemplative prayer seemed to be in his caring for others.[11]

When Pope Paul VI proclaimed St. Teresa of Jesus (Avila) the first woman Doctor of the Church, September 27, 1970, he chose the title: "Teresa of Avila, Teacher of Prayer." St. Teresa explained the practice of prayer in her three major works: *The Life of St. Teresa of Jesus of the Order of Our Lady of the Carmel Written by Herself*, *The Way of Perfection*, and *The Interior Castle*. Even with such masterpieces, it was not easy for Teresa to get to the "better part" and God helped her with her struggle. As Fr. Dubay stated:

> Yet Teresa had her faults, for saints are not born out of the blue. They are weighed down with the same weak human nature we all have and they experience the same temptations.[12]

Fr. Dubay recounts the spiritual story of Teresa who, though she had a good mind, lacked formal education. The master general of the Carmelite Order authorized her, at the age of 52, to found reformed houses of Carmelite men and women. Because the original copy of the *Book of Her Life* was confiscated during the Inquisition, her spiritual director exhorted her to write a book of the Dwelling Places (John 14:2), which she began on Holy Trinity Sunday, June 2, 1577. God showed her instantly the whole book and gave her the image of a castle.

Teresa writes:

> Today while beseeching our Lord to speak for me because I wasn't able to think of anything to say nor did I know how to begin to carry out this obedience, there came to my mind what I shall now speak about, that which will provide us with a basis to begin with. It is that we consider our soul to be like a castle made entirely out of a diamond or of very clear crystal, in which there are many rooms, just as in heaven there are many dwelling places. For in reflecting upon it carefully, Sisters, we realized that the soul of the just person is nothing else but a paradise where the Lord says he finds his delight.[13]

At the center of the castle was the King of Glory in splendor, illuminating all the dwelling places to the outer wall. The spiritual life inside the castle was complex with differing spiritual depths which indicated an individual's capacities, and prayer became the opening as one advanced from the first prayer place to the seventh, with transformative union in the seventh place. St. Teresa seems pre-occupied more with the last four dwelling places where God is more active and the prayer more passive. She seems to give no advice about methods.

One enters the first dwelling place with occasional prayer, even if the soul is very much engaged with the world and possessions. The soul encounters the mystery of God in the castle and will continue to grow with more self-knowledge and humility.

Humility is important to St. Teresa. Humility expands the soul. She maintained that detachment from oneself—from worry about esteem and honor—is alongside humility. And with more perseverance in prayer, the soul is growing through good books, and homilies.

"What I have come to understand," remarks Teresa, "is that this whole groundwork of prayer is based on humility and that the more a soul lowers itself in prayer, the more God raises it up."[14]

In the first dwelling place, there is distraction during these occasions of prayer. In *30 Days with Teresa of Avila,* Dan Burke and Anthony Lilles stated that St. Teresa said not to worry about distractions. They quote from her letters:

Do not tire your brain by trying to work it during meditation. It is a higher grace from God that you should continually praise him and wish that others should do so too, so that your mind is fixed on him. [15]

According to Burke and Lilles, Teresa discourages the person who prays from being attached to thinking or feeling much mental prayer. In *The Book of the Foundations of Teresa of Jesus, Written by Herself*, St. Teresa stated: "The good of the soul does not consist in thinking but in its loving much." [16] She emphasizes that we should simply surrender and trust and be vulnerable to the presence of the Lord. If we continue to analyze or imagine what is happening, then we may have difficulty going within.

Initially, especially with beginners, the thinking, feeling, and distractions during contemplative prayer are numerous. In addition to the distractions, one can get stuck in analyzing what is going on, rather than simply experiencing the moment. One can actually ask the questions of himself: "What is happening right now?" "How long have I been silent?" "How much more time is left in my time cycle?" "Am I doing this correctly?" "What am I feeling right now?" And others.

Because of the tendency toward mental activity, the person may miss the experience and then become discouraged. Therefore, I usually recommend beginning with small increments of silence, like five or ten minutes at first, and build up to longer. At first, starting with even five or ten minutes can seem like a very long time.

And I have learned that it's important to keep a consecutive, daily time for quiet with the Lord. I notice that if I miss

a few days because of busyness, I often have to "build up" the
time again. Like an athlete who gets out of shape, you have
to work back up to a certain training level to feel the effects.

† † †

While we were vacationing in Hawaii once, I had no
alone time for about a week. I was concerned that I could not
recollect or find quiet within myself to encounter God.
When I returned home, I began the "build-up" again, in
somewhat small increments. My recollection time returned
quickly; I believe that God works with us to restore that part
of our relationship with him. We can ask him to help us to
retrieve it.

St. Teresa of Jesus (Avila) had a fragile nature and a mind
that was alert and active, and she was subject to digression.
She felt tormented over the inability to concentrate. In fact,
she would often fall asleep when she was praying. She said
the Lord taught her things such as *Lectio Divina* and other
prayer strategies. For instance, Teresa would *represent* him
within herself. But she is not referring to some vivid pictur-
ing—within her imagination or to the composition of place
with all its detail. Her concern is not with the physical details
of the physical qualities of Christ or of the particular scene.

For Teresa, "representing Christ" had more to do with
becoming aware of his presence, and becoming present to

him, as he is never taking his eyes off us. She goes directly to the person of Christ in his humanity, and she brings him to her consciousness as either within her or beside her.

At this point, the soul is persevering in prayer, and there is movement into the second dwelling place. However, because there is greater desire for God, the enemy begins to wage a fierce war against the soul, reminding the soul of the pleasures and honor the soul formerly experienced outside the castle (outside the first dwelling place). Teresa stated that it was important that the soul not give up on prayer but ask God's mercy so as not to fall or linger behind.

In this second dwelling place, there is more reception to God's grace through a "prayer of acquired recollection." In *The Way of Perfection*, written at the direction of her confessor sometime before 1567, she wrote about active/acquired recollection. She distinguished between "active" or "acquired" versus the "passive recollection," which is found primarily in the fourth dwelling place. In passive recollection, commonly known as infused recollection, a mystical experience is taking place with God; and again, this is more common in the fourth dwelling place.

In acquired recollection, we are doing the work, to shift our focus to the things of God and our coming into his presence. We use our intellects, our imaginations, and our hearts to reflect on the holy scriptures (as in *Lectio Divina* or otherwise); we also use holy icons, spiritual writings, the rosary, or other prayers. We are turning away from earthly things to move into a dimension of stillness and quiet where we can hear God. We ignore the exterior senses, and we avoid attention to them. Meanwhile, the soul is expanding; it is easier to find God within as the separation occurs.

Effort and determination occupy us, as we let him take away the things that are not of him. Teresa states that as we desire the prayer of recollection, we will acquire more self-control and overcome the senses. It is the vanities of the world that can get in the way of our recollection.

In my spiritual life, I initially struggled, and sometimes still struggle, with multiple distractions—both externally and internally. Early, it was difficult to stay silent and await the Lord's presence by separating myself from tasks and people. When practicing the Carmelite daily "Rule of Life," which includes 30 minutes of mental prayer, those 30 minutes seemed very long and exhaustive at times.

As I mentioned previously, to calm my inner self and to keep from being overwhelmed, I began silent prayer in small increments, even as little as five minutes of the thirty minutes, to be present to Christ. As I examined myself, I became clear on my personality patterns, and I found I was vulnerable to greater distraction by late afternoon. Morning appeared to be best for my mental and contemplative prayer schedule.

Focusing on particular prayers, like the Divine Mercy Chaplet or rosary, scripture (*Lectio Divina* at times), or a homily from an early morning Mass enhanced my solitude and quiet. I retreated to my "spiritual corner" with bibles, commentaries, spiritual books, statues, spiritual icons, and other relics.

As I mentioned previously, an especially meaningful relic is a framed flower from the home garden at the residence of St. Therese of Lisieux, one of her favorite places. Some years ago, I walked through that garden while visiting the house where she grew up. When I think of a God of love, she is one of those models of love; and she inspires me with her teachings on love.

In chapter XI of *Story of a Soul Study Edition*, prepared by Fr. Marc Foley, O.C.D., she wrote of her *vocation of love*.

Sometimes, like St. Teresa, I am inclined to think that I am "representing" Christ within me with a memory from the Holy Land. Some years ago, when my husband and I went on pilgrimage there, I recall going out on the Mediterranean Sea in a boat much like the boat Jesus would have used—a very simple one. Then we walked the seashore, picking up small shells to bring home. In prayer, I can still see and feel the water and the seashore, where I collected shells and where Jesus walked. I can tenderly picture Jesus there–in the boat and on the seashore.

Another place that is full of silence and can provide a significant meeting with God is in a Eucharistic Adoration Chapel or sitting before the Blessed Sacrament in an empty Church. The presence of God is so concrete in the Eucharist. Immediately upon being near the Eucharist, the mind and body quiet. As I mentioned previously, practice makes it easier to settle in.

It is interesting that habit forms, or *habituation* takes place, with *sameness–same* time, *same* place and *same* process. Some examples of habituation can help illustrate:

When we enter a room, we might feel distracted by a noisy air conditioner, but as we spend more time in the room, we soon lose our attention toward it; although it is still present, it does not cause concern or tension. This process happens naturally or unconsciously, so we don't have to make it happen.

Routine is another example. I think of my elementary school process of coming home from school, having a snack, then playing outside. I would also go to the same desk in my room around the same time and do my homework. This schedule was re-enforced by my mother for a while; and then it became easier, a routine. Since it was expected, I did it and found that I had less resistance in body and mind, as time went on.

It is the same for prayer, I believe.

With psychotherapy clients, I used to offer a relaxation therapy technique. I used this technique so often that I became *habituated* to it. In the first few minutes of my instruction to the client to get comfortable in the chair, relax their muscles and change their breathing, I found that I also became comfortable and began to yawn and was noticeably (to me) relaxed.

In *Interior Castle*, St. Teresa of Jesus (Avila) said one becomes habituated and acquired recollection occurs more quickly as they enter the third dwelling place in the soul through prayer. In this place, a soul is careful not to offend God; they seek to do penance, make time for charitable works, and avoid committing even venial sins. Doing the will of the Father is very important.

Again, as one keeps praying regularly, he may enter the fourth dwelling place, considered the beginning of contemplative prayer and mystical prayer. Here the Lord brings the person into his presence through *infused recollection*, where there is an awareness of the Lord's love that is flowing in the quiet and stillness.

Since the Lord has taken over, this movement into the stillness, quiet, and love can occur unexpectedly. One feels a "touch of God," with the desire to make room for this moment. For me, in the early moments of mental prayer and silence, that "touch of God" can occur in a flash. One minute I may be praying some rote prayers, like the *Liturgy of the Hours*, and then I feel stopped from that direction. It literally feels as if a stop sign is put in front of me. All of a sudden, I am going in a different direction, and I cannot go on my own speed. There are no words or thinking.

† † †

Since my trip to Medjugorje, and renewed consecration to Our Blessed Mother, I find that she will often lead me to the "doorstep" of contemplation. It is as if I am magnetized by her love, as I feel led to place a blessed picture of her over my heart. I am drawn into a moment where I am stilled and feel at one with Jesus. When I experience any difficulty recollecting myself, I know that I can count on Our Lady to direct me to her Son.

Fr. Dubay quoted St. Teresa and better explained it:

> "Often when a person is quite unprepared for such a thing and is not even thinking of God, he is awakened by his majesty as though by a rushing comet or thunderclap. The soul is aware that it is called by God."

> Teresa got in touch with this and called it drinking of the living waters and how God satisfies and takes away the thirst for earthly things. It is like a "divine inflow."[17]

Fr. Dubay wrote that at times this is a delightful loving attention, at times a dry purifying desire and at other times a strong thirsting for him. In the beginning, it is usually delicate and brief but as it develops it becomes burning powerful, absorbing and prolonged. One Discalced Carmelite I know has described the experience of God's drawing her inward as a sort of "absorption." Another reported feeling that all was "quiet within."

In *Fulfillment of All Desire*, Ralph Martin said St. Teresa describes the beginning of infused contemplation or recollection as a "hearing" or "being drawn" by God to open to His presence and pay attention.[18]

It is not a matter of imagining being with Him or thinking about the truth of the interior indwelling—although these are good elements of meditation as they are founded on the important truth of God being within us—but of an almost imperceptible interior hearing of the gentle whisper. This is a wonderful place, spiritually, as one progresses along the pathway of prayer to closeness with God. And yet, God will then move the prayer forward.

Martin writes that St. Teresa also speaks of the degrees of infused contemplation in the fourth dwelling place.[19] There is the "Prayer of Quiet," a way to pray, which captivates the will, although other faculties will be free. She writes that the soul is satisfied with God, as long as the recollection lasts, as the will is united with God, even though the will brings the intellect and memory back to recollection and the will is still content.

Fr. Dubay stated that focus on the indwelling presence helps to be ready for the Prayer of Quiet.[20]

A more intense form of the Prayer of Quiet is the "sleep of the faculties," where the other faculties in addition to the will are under the rule of the Lord in prayer. In a metaphor, the water is coming to the garden by ways of rivers and streams that flow into the garden.[21]

In *The Way of Perfection,* Teresa notes that the Lord often gives small "pledges" or "little sips" of what will be given in abundance in the kingdom.

> But there are times when, tired from our travels, we experience that the Lord calms our faculties and quiets the soul. As though by signs, He gives us a clear foretaste of what will be given to those He brings to His kingdom... Those who experience this prayer call it the prayer of quiet. [22]

She uses the term "perfect contemplation" to refer to those pure forms of contemplation found in the fifth, sixth, and seventh dwelling places. She explains about the dissimilarities between perfect contemplation and mental prayer. Mental prayer is understanding what is explained and knowing who is speaking to you. We can think of many things and also how much we need to serve him and how little we have actually served him. We can do something with God's help. She states: "In the contemplation I now mentioned; we can do nothing. His Majesty is the one who does everything, for it is his work and above our nature." [23]

At the center of the castle is God's dwelling place and union occurs through a series of degrees of contemplation. As one moves then into the fifth, sixth, and seventh dwelling places, the mystical elements of the spiritual life are seen, such as the Prayer of Union in which the will, the memory, imagination, and the intellect are absorbed by the Lord, as if suspended, and there is deep absorption in the Lord. [24]

In *The Way of Perfection*, St. Teresa has a stern warning for those who do not want to advance in prayer:

> Therefore, daughters if you desire that I tell you about the way that leads to contemplation, you will have to bear with me if I enlarge a little on some other matters even though they may not seem to you so important; for in my opinion, they are. And if you don't want to hear about them or put them in to practice, stay with your mental prayer for your whole life, for I assure you and all persons who aim after true contemplation (through I could be mistaken since I am judging by myself for whom it took twenty years) that you will not thereby reach it. [25]

† † †

Feeling the presence of God in prayer is a very consoling experience. And yet, in *The Dark Night: Psychological Experience and Spiritual Reality*, Fr. Marc Foley, O.C.D., writes of the fading of God's consolation in beginning prayer. He said although consolation from God helped wean people from their external attachments and attached them to God, at some point, the Lord will begin a process of detaching us from the consolations. This is called "the passive night of sense," as purification occurs in the ego and in the senses. It is the first "purgation" with the second being "the dark night of the spirit."

Fr. Marc points out:

> ...this does not mean that God has withdrawn; rather, the mode of the inflow of God has changed from consolation to contemplation. This means that the dark night is not devoid of God's presence.[26]

Experiencing the presence of God with emotions, a remembrance of a scripture, or just the feel of a loving presence, provides the one who prays with a certain security of knowing God is there and that prayer is not in vain.

When this is removed, as in the *dark night of the senses,* one can think of his/her prayer as "dry." It can be confusing, as it is so different from the usual time of prayer. It feels as if God is not present, although this is not the case. When the consolation of his reassuring presence is taken away, it can make a person wonder, *What does this mean?*

In my experiences, I sit and wait on God, expecting consolation. When it does not happen, I also wonder. Yet Fr. Foley maintains that God is leading the soul higher in prayer. He said, "The mode of the inflow of God has changed from consolation to contemplation. That *night* is contemplation."[27]

That means I have to make the decision to sit with God, even when I don't "feel" his presence. Again, Fr. Foley states that God is present to the soul differently than before; and we have to move out of our "attachment" to the sensual experience and make room for the spirit.

In that moment, we are being called to experience God alone and quietly; and this is a higher level of the contemplative experience. As St. Teresa would point out: It is good to understand where we are in prayer (the dwelling place), so that we don't turn away or give up. We need to get to the point that we just want to be still with God, and feelings no longer matter.

As we continue to cultivate a non-possessive attitude while trying to make meditation work and just be in God's loving attention, we can relax and let God draw us into silence.

In Fr. Marc Foley's *The Dark Night*, he makes the point that transformation is occurring, but we cannot feel it, and can wonder if our prayer will ever have the fervor it once had. He said:

> This is one of the paradoxes of the dark night. When our soul has become submerged in grace, we feel that God is absent. Nevertheless, we still experience God, not in the imagination, the intellect, or the memory but in our desire for God. [28]

There is much more to say here, but what seems most *poignant* is the thirst to feel God's presence in the *old* way. We yearn and desire him; and yet, in this "dry" experience, we have to accept patiently, trusting that a *new* movement of God is at work. Still, it feels like a death of sorts, and we can mourn, wishing for the old relationship.

In my own experience, it is a darkness, wanting to know he is there and yet not knowing because all consolations are gone. I often ask, "Where are you God?" and "Could you speak to me and let me know what you are thinking about the situations I bring to you?"

In the many years I've enjoyed a daily connection and foundation with Jesus, I still suffer without "feeling" his previous consoling presence. And yet I know I have to wait, letting God transform my soul. It is difficult to wait in his perceived absence.

I must trust in scripture and the truth it brings: that God is always with us. As Matthew 28:20 reminds us:

> ....teaching them to observe all that I have commanded you; and behold I am with you always until the end of the age.

As explained above, it is in our *yearning* for him that we know that we are connected and still connecting. Through that, we can be encouraged.

According to Fr. Marc Foley, in the transformation, the

presence of God purifies us and is an undoing of our built-up habits so that what was once in the darkness can come to the light of love and be converted.

I think that this must have been the case with St. Teresa of Calcutta, Mother Teresa. We witnessed her work from afar, her compassion, and selflessness. In *Mother Teresa: Come Be My Light*, Fr. Brian Kolodiejchuk, M.C., editor, reminds us that Mother Teresa often said:

> Very often I feel like a little pencil in God's Hands. He does the writing, He does the thinking, He does the movement, I have only to be the pencil." (from Mother Teresa's speech in Rome, March 7, 1979).[29]

And Mother Teresa was sure that using her nothingness would bring out his greatness. Fr. Kolodiejchuk points out that she was so well known for her public work, and yet she kept her interior life and relationship with God hidden, out of reverence and love for him.

Fr. Kolodiejchuk wrote that Mother Teresa's mission to serve the poor came at a "cost" and that she would be in darkness that was intense. Following her death, it became known that Mother Teresa suffered in the darkness of not hearing God's voice. She lived in a spiritual desert and felt that God had rejected her. From 1946 to 1997, she did not feel the presence of God, yet she glowed with his love and mercy to the poor she served in Calcutta and to those around the world.

In his book *The Love That Made Mother Teresa* David Scott told of her 1957 confession to her spiritual director:

> In the darkness...Lord, my God, who am I that you should forsake me? ....The one you have thrown away as unwanted—unloved. I call, I cling, I want, and there is no one to answer...Where I try to raise my thoughts to heaven, there is such convicting emptiness that those very thoughts return like sharp knives and hurt my very soul. Love—the word—it brings nothing. I am told God lives in me, and yet the reality of darkness and coldness and emptiness is so great that nothing touches my soul. [30]

And yet this confession remained private, and the world embraced her goodness and mercy. David Scott likens her suffering to those for whom she served—the poor, the unwanted children, the atheist who can't say prayers or feel love. He wrote that she seemed to bear their sufferings, the sufferings of Christ.

He further reports that she seemed to understand that the darkness was a divine trial. She made a private vow of spiritual espousal—to give all to Jesus and not to refuse him. According to Scott, Jesus was claiming Mother Teresa for himself and pruning her self-love and pride, purifying her heart, mind, and intention, taking away anything that would hinder her total union with him. Was this a *dark night* of the soul, as defined by St. John of the Cross, a purification so that love could come forward more perfectly?

As I think of my own experiences in times of darkness in contemplative prayer, I am encouraged by Mother Teresa, who was steadfast in her love and promises to God to serve the poorest of the poor, no matter what the trials—and to the end of her life.

In marital counseling, I often told my couples that loving behavior at times might not be backed by feelings, so it needed to be, simply, a behavioral decision. The foundation of a sacramental marriage, built upon commitment to one another and to God for a lifetime of love, was sustaining no matter the trials. And it was a choice to live this out.

Just as it is a choice to stay with God, in the silence, in the seemingly absent voice, as he brings each life to perfection in him.

CHAPTER 8

Receiving from a Mother's Heart and Prayer

Receiving love from our Blessed Mother Mary's heart is a touch I need many times daily. I begin this chapter, however, sharing gifts I received from a person who was like a second earthly mother to me. We called her "Tott," and she had a heart that kept caring.

Perhaps the Blessed Mother gave Tott to me with a special purpose in mind, as she filled my childhood years with love and tenderness. Tott has passed on, but my spiritual mother, Mary, continues to be with me and bless me.

Tott was the mother of my neighborhood friends who lived two doors down—Betsy and her younger sister, Marie. The two of them, plus Mary Nell (another friend), my sister and I walked to school together and played in the woods around our houses daily; we were inseparable. Although Betsy and Marie were our daily playmates, Tott fit in like a playmate as well as a mother.

She taught us how to sew, embroider, knit, and make a milkshake that tasted so good, you didn't have to add ice cream. Tott didn't shoo us away, like some mothers. She liked spending time with us. We created and performed plays at Tott and her husband Abe's home, and she allowed us to invite and charge our neighbors admission to the shows. It was such fun!

In her motherly care, she was comforting, patient, and unconditionally loving. After my sister and I were grown, Tott met us for lunch, occasionally, when we came to town. And in-between trips, she sent us tender notes of love, including little gifts of bracelets or socks—whatever was on her heart and that she could get out to purchase. Probably the most touching gift I received was a monthly copy of her Methodist magazine—the large print edition! Now, that's a mother with a heart for you.

I recall accepting the Virgin Mary as my "spiritual mother," literally, at the moment I heard a talk given by a Dominican sister at a Charismatic Conference. The talk was entitled: "Mary as Role Model." It was my first Charismatic Conference, and the first talk I'd ever heard on Mary, and something just clicked inside.

Since I was raised Presbyterian, I knew little about Mary's role in salvation history. As I listened to Sister Jean talk, I suddenly realized her significance in a way I could not explain. And it seemed as though I knew Mary *personally*, from a long-time relationship. In that instant, I loved her and took her into my heart—no questions asked.

I became Mary's child then and I have continued to follow her call into "more" with her as well as her Son, Jesus. But understanding the origin of this "instant love" and acceptance came several years later, at a Catholic conference in Santa Fe, New Mexico. And understanding her significance in the lives of all so that salvation history would change came later as well. More on this story later.

I have since come to believe that the Blessed Mother wants to be our mother, as well as role model. She wants to add our "yes" to her "yes" in what God asks of us. She said "yes," when she was greeted by the archangel Gabriel, who revealed God's plan for her. And she responded, "I am the handmaid of the Lord. May it be done to me according to your word" (Luke 1:38).

At the Charismatic conference, I found my "yes" led me to recognition of and devotion to her as well as a movement into a more personal relationship with Jesus. I had read no books and knew nothing intellectually about the Blessed Mother, but the bond was there.

My heart had already connected powerfully to the Holy Spirit a year earlier. I had joined a Catholic Charismatic prayer group and now recognized the personhood of the Holy Spirit and the magnitude of the Holy Spirit, as guide to Jesus' teachings.

As we know, Mary is also considered the "spouse" of the Holy Spirit. Fr. Michael Gaitley in *33 Days to Morning Glory*, comments:

When Mary said, 'Behold, I am the handmaid of the Lord; let it be done to me according to you word' (Luke 1:38), we can see most clearly that she's the spouse of the Holy Spirit, for at that moment, she gave the Holy Spirit permission to conceive Christ in her womb. Thus, at that moment the already unfathomably deep bond between Mary and the Holy Spirit that had begun (in time) at the first moment of her Immaculate Conception was revealed as nothing less than a two-become-one marital union (See Gen. 2:24). As a result of that union, the Holy Spirit is pleased to work and act through his spouse, Mary, for the sanctification of the human race.[1]

Saying "yes" to the Holy Spirit and recognizing his personhood and role, I was also recognizing Mary as spouse of the Holy Spirit. The two were inseparable.

† † †

In 1984, my colleagues and I were on our way to a retreat center outside Mexico City to attend the international conference of the Association of Christian Therapists. While we met annually, this particular event was significant, as we were given time to visit the Shrine of Our Lady of Guadalupe in Mexico City. Our Association priests celebrated Mass there, in front of the actual Tilma of Juan Diego, and we were privileged to be able to get very close to the framed tilma.

The reverence of the Mexican people was so beautiful and inspiring. Many would not even turn their back on the Blessed Mother's picture/image; they would leave the church on their knees, backing up, showing reverence as they departed.

I love the intimate story of (now Saint) Juan Diego, and his "yes" to the Blessed Mother. His story is very real, perhaps, like ours would be, if the Blessed Mother appeared to us and asked us to go on a mission for which we felt unprepared and unworthy. Juan Diego was just a little soul, like us. Would we be in awe and fear, as he was, if we were also called into a great mission?

In *Meetings with Mary: Visions of the Blessed Mother*, Janice T. Connell tells the story of this 57-year-old Indian man who received apparitions from the Blessed Mother in December 1431 in Mexico. When she appeared to him on Tepeyac Hill, Our Lady told Juan Diego in his mother tongue, that she was "the ever-virgin Mary, Mother of the true God who gives life and maintains it in existence."[2] She said that the Lord desired that a temple or church be built there "where your people may experience my compassion." She said further: "All who sincerely ask my help in their work in and in their sorrows will know my Mother's Heart in this place."[3] She would see their tears and she would console them, and they would be at peace.

Then the Blessed Mother sent him on a mission to the Bishop to tell him all that he had seen and heard. Juan Diego told the Bishop Zumaraga (who had great love for the Blessed Mother) what he had seen and heard, and added the request of the Blessed Mother, which was to build a basilica on Tepeyac Hill. The bishop said he would consider this but did not act on it.

Juan Diego, in tears, returned to Tepeyac Hill, relating to the Blessed Mother that he had failed in the mission she had given him. Our Lady instructed Juan Diego to return to the Bishop and express her desires.

The Bishop, in this next visit, was not enthusiastic, wanting a sign from the Blessed Mother to confirm the story he heard. Juan Diego reported to the Blessed Mother, who told him not to fear and that she would give the Bishop the sign he needed and that he was to return to that spot the next day.

Juan failed to return the next day, as his uncle was mortally ill; and he stayed to care for him. Haven't we all made choices that kept us from following what the Blessed Mother and our Lord wanted? No worries, Mary through Jesus gives us a second opportunity, as she did with Juan Diego.

When Juan Diego passed by Tepeyac Hill, Mary was waiting for him.

> Do not be distressed and afraid, my littlest son. Am I not here with you who am your Mother? Are you not under my shadow and protection?[4]

How many times does our mother Mary come to us and remind us who she is and that we are under her protection? Then, she invites us into the *mission* of the work of salvation, interceding to bring souls to Jesus.

Juan Diego was told further that his uncle would not die but be restored to health, and that he should go and cut some roses (they were out of season at the time, another miracle). Juan Diego carried the Castilian roses in his tilma (cloak) to the Blessed Mother, who rearranged the bouquets and said that this was the sign for the Bishop. She called Juan Diego her "trusted ambassador" and assured him this time the Bishop would believe him.

The bishop opened the tilma and the Castilian roses fell out. On the tilma itself there was a full-length image of the Blessed Virgin Mary. To this day, that image remains. It is the only divine image of the Blessed Virgin Mary that appears on earth; it's framed and housed in the basilica in Mexico City, and she is now known as Our Lady of Guadalupe.

Mary asks all of us the same questions she asked Juan Diego: "Am I not your Mother? Are you not under my shadow and protection?" And so, I ask myself the question that she asked of him and answer in the affirmative. Yes, she is my mother, and I am in the shadow of her protection. No matter what she asks of me, I can trust her to take care of me.

† † †

In *St. John Paul the Great: His Five Loves,* Jason Evert writes of the Pope's devotion to the Blessed Mother. As a young man in Poland, Karol Wojtyla would walk to and from work with the book by St. Louis de Montfort, *True Devotion to Mary.* He learned through this book that "Mary leads us to Christ" and "Christ leads us to Mary."[5]

After reading the book, the Pope (now saint) made the consecration to Mary, which was a transforming moment in his life. He later entrusted his pontificate to her with the words: "Totus Tuus," totally yours. Fr. Michael Gaitley reminds us of the basis for John Paul II's consecration to Mary.

Archbishop Fulton J. Sheen in *The Cries of Jesus from the Cross: An Anthology* says that Mary stood by her Son at the Cross, and she never let Him go. He writes:

> Behold thy son! It was the second Nativity! Mary had brought her first-born without labor, in the cave of Bethlehem; she now brings forth her second-born, John, in the labors of the Cross. At this moment Mary is undergoing the pains of childbirth, not only for her second-born who is John, but also for the millions who will be born to her in Christian ages as "Children of Mary."[6]

He writes that Christ was her first born and that it was not that she was to have other children by the blood of flesh, but that she was to have other children by the blood of her heart. Mary never let Jesus go; and she will never let us go. She is God's special instrument to bring souls to Jesus, and when you take her into your heart, she brings you to Jesus and to his mission for you.

With Mary at the foot of the cross, Jesus tells her, "Woman, behold your son." He is entrusting all peoples to her motherly care. Then when he speaks to St. John the Evangelist, who represents all peoples, Jesus says: "Behold, your mother."

Fr. Michael Gaitley further reminds us that in the main teachings of Vatican II in the last chapter of the Dogmatic Constitution of the church, *Lumen Gentium*, Mary's role is explained—that she is with us in her "maternal mediation."[7] In other words, she prays for us and nurtures us to move us closer to God.

Dr. Mark Miravalle, president of the International Marian Association, and St. John Paul II Chair of Mariology at Franciscan University of Steubenville, gives us a better understanding in his lecture entitled: "Mary Mother of All Peoples," which is included in the DVD series "That Man is You." He speaks of the four dogmas of Mary: The Mother of God, her perpetual virginity, her immaculate conception, and her assumption. These four dogmas offer us the truth about Mary that is central to the Catholic faith. He points out, however, that these dogmas do not explain Mary's relationship to each of us.

I happened to watch this DVD with my husband, as I often am drawn to Mary when I have the opportunity to know her better. His men's group, "That Man is You," was viewing and would be discussing the video. As I watched and listened, I was surprised to learn of a fifth "doctrine" not "dogma" as of yet, that gave credence to our relationship with Mary as spiritual mother. He explains that even though it's an official doctrine it has not been solemnly defined by the Pope.

There are two ways that doctrines become dogmas: an infallible statement by the Holy Father or coming out of an ecumenical council and confirmed by the Holy Father.

Dr. Miravalle states that what is taught by the papal Magisterium of the church is that Mary is our spiritual mother, but it is not yet a solemn doctrine. As we know from John 19:25-27, we are all given the gift of Mary as mother by Jesus, as was the disciple, John. As John took her into his "home," we are also given the same instruction. Dr. Miravalle states that there is no Greek translation for "home" but rather it is translated "own."

So, we are to take Mary into our own hearts and spiritual life. It is a "theological" fact that we are given Mary as gift and that we should not reject this gift, given by Jesus. So, he asks us to consider the questions, how do we "properly behold" Mary as our mother? In her spiritual motherhood, she acts as mother: as co-redemptrix, mediatrix of all graces, and advocate. In these roles, she suffers with us, as she did with

Jesus (but is not on an equal level with Jesus), she nourishes us with the graces of redemption, and pleads for us and defends us.

† † †

Fr. Michael Gaitley points out that John Paul II spoke of the "New motherhood of Mary" as "the fruits of the 'new' love which developed into a conclusive maturity at the foot of the cross."[8] Further, Mother Teresa espoused that Mary was the one who took Jesus' words "I thirst" into her heart and she brings others to her heart as well. It is out of this new development of Mary's motherhood that we learn she is aflame with Jesus' love for those for whom he suffered and died: her mission.

I realize that as I accept the *gift* of Mary as my spiritual mother, not only do I accept her *maternal mediation* and *protection*, but that I accept the *mission* of bringing suffering souls to Christ.

And it seemed that the mission of bringing suffering souls to Christ was to happen not as a member of the Presbyterian church, but as a Catholic. After two years of spiritual struggle and in the agony of indecision, one morning, while washing my hands, out of the blue, I had an image in my mind's eye of a perfectly formed rosary. I was startled. It was beautiful; and then it went away, just as quickly as it had occurred. Never had I experienced anything of this magnitude, later learning that this was called an "infused contemplation."[9]

The experience seemed to me to be the "sign" that I was to join the Catholic church. Mary as well as the Holy Spirit were beckoning me into the church—a step in the call to mission? I wondered. I joined the Catholic church, with no reservation, grateful for my Presbyterian heritage, and ready for the "more" into which I was being directed.

As I stated earlier, when I received the Eucharist for the first time that July morning, after a few months of instruction by the pastor, I "knew that I knew," as they say, that I had for the first time consumed "the real presence of Jesus Christ." I now understood that I was led by the Blessed Mother and the Holy Spirit into this "more" of the faith journey and mission.

In *33 Days*, Fr. Michael Gaitley writes:

> So, it is Mary's great God-given task, in union with and by the power of the Holy Spirit, to form every human being into 'another Christ,' that is to unite everyone to the Body of Christ and form each person into a fully mature member of the body. [10]

Part of that maturation for me occurred when I felt called on pilgrimage to Medjugorje, Yugoslavia, where it was purported that the Blessed Mother was appearing to six children. When I read *Medjugorje, the Message* by journalist Wayne Weible, there was no question that she was calling me there, just as she had called him.

Since Yugoslavia, at that time, was a Communist country, our 1989 trip was beset with intimidation tactics by the Communists, and it was scary. At one airport, our suitcases were thoroughly searched, and our leaders were held back by the guards to go on a separate plane. The Blessed Mother protected us, so after our leaders re-joined us and an additional two-hour bus ride, we arrived safely in the little village of Medjugorje. We felt secure, as we stayed in a Catholic family's home and were surrounded by the villagers who were also devoutly Catholic.

My then twelve-year-old daughter was with me, and there were several children and teenagers on the trip. One night, the youth went with the tour director to the house of Vicka, who had a nightly visitation. My daughter particularly desired to go and take our silver medals along. I immediately said yes, and indeed a miracle occurred. My Sacred Heart of Jesus silver medal turned to gold.

While the children were at Vicka's, the adults arrived at St. James Parish for Mass. Once seated there, worrisome thoughts and questions filled my mind: *I let her go with the tour guide and I really do not know him. I do not know where she is, and what if something happens? She may look for me and not be able to find me. What should I do?*

Finally, I decided to trust the Blessed Mother and continue to focus on the Mass and the Eucharist. My daughter returned that night to the home where we were staying, and she was thrilled that the medal turned to gold. Now, she could show this miracle to her class. The best part: My sixth grader was convinced of the appearance of the Blessed Mother, and so were her classmates.

Years later, I would also point to this miracle as a confirmation for my decision to join the Third Order Discalced Carmelites.

† † †

Mirjana Soldo is one of the original six visionaries who, beginning in 1981, received apparitions of the Blessed Mother in Medjugorje. In her book *My Heart Will Triumph*, she records one of our Lady's messages to her from March 18, 2011:

> My children, do not be afraid to open your hearts to me. With motherly love, I will show you what I expect of each of you, what I expect of my apostles. Set out with me.[11]

Later, the Blessed Mother names those who open their hearts to her as "apostles" and, more recently, "apostles of love." She continues to "draw us to her," just as she did Pope John Paul II.

There have been many appearances of the Blessed Mother on the earth for centuries. And as stated in *The Catechism of the Catholic Church*:

> This motherhood of Mary in the order of grace continues uninterruptedly from the consent which she loyally gave at the Annunciation and which she sustained without wavering beneath the cross, until the eternal fulfillment of all the elect. Taken up to heaven she did not lay aside this saving office but by her manifold intercession continues to bring us the gifts of eternal salvation....Therefore, the Blessed Virgin is invoked in the church under the titles of Advocate, Helper, Benefactress, and Mediatrix (*CCC*, 969).

In Janice T. Connell's *Meetings with Mary*, she chronicles the many appearances from 1522 Manresa, Spain, to Ignatius Loyola and beyond under the titles of Mary: "Queen of All Saints," "Mother of Divine Grace," "Queen of the Holy Rosary," "Queen of Peace," "Mother of the Word" "Mother of Good Counsel," "Queen of Angels," "Mother of All Nations and All People," and "Mother of Divine Mercy."

In his foreword to that book, Fr. Robert Faricy, S.J., writes of the purposes of Mary's appearances, whether to a few persons or a whole locality or even for the world. The church investigates each appearance and may or may not approve. He says:

> Church approval after thorough and stringent evaluation, means that official experts have examined the event carefully, and that they have found nothing false. We can therefore accept these events as true. [12]

He says that she appears as "mother" and that is what she is—our mother. Jesus gave her to us!

I had a special and quite unexpected experience of Mary as "mother" in Sante Fe, New Mexico at the conference I mentioned in the first part of this chapter. I was the "baby" Catholic in the group—still learning, being fed spiritually, and on fire with the faith.

In the Catholic conference, there was the characteristic "laying on of hands" [13] praying. One of the ladies with whom I had made the journey prayed over me and reported that she had a vision of me as an infant, and the Blessed Mother was nursing me. It seemed that my mother could not produce enough breast milk. My friend said that Mary was "literally" saving me in the first six months of life. At this, I broke down crying, actually sobbing.

Then there was an awakening. I flashed back to my experience of the Charismatic Conference and the talk by the Dominican sister on the Blessed Mother, when I accepted Mary as my mother. Through knowledge that only the Holy Spirit could give, I realized that, as an infant, I had known Mary in those early months. She was familiar to my spirit for this reason. She kept me alive, as a mother, feeding me and nurturing me, and "mediating" me, as previously defined by Fr. Michael Gaitley. And in those early months, I bonded with her—developmentally and spiritually, as babies do with their mothers. So, no wonder there was "instant love" at that conference! Now, I was re-connecting to her as the Holy Spirit enlightened me.

My current home is in the St. Augustine, Florida, area, and I go occasionally to the National Shrine of Our Lady of La Leche (translated as Our Lady of the Milk and of the Good and Happy Childbirth). Mary is shown nursing Jesus, and I am drawn to this image of Mary, which now makes sense to me because of my experience with Mary in my infancy.

St. Augustine is considered to be the oldest city on the North American continent, and it possesses the oldest Catholic parish in the United States, dating back to 1594. It is recorded that General Don Pedro Menendez de Aviles and his sailors came from Spain to the New World in hopes of establishing a colony and securing the land for Spain. On September 8, the feast day of the nativity of the Blessed Virgin Mary, the Spanish on the ships, sailors, priests, and others came to shore. It was recorded that Father Francisco Lopez de Mendoza Grajales took a cross and went to meet the General singing the hymn "Te Deum Laudamus." The General went to the Cross, knelt and kissed it, and the Indians who watched imitated this behavior.

This land was proclaimed in the Name of God (Nombre de Dios), and Mass was celebrated. It was on this sacred ground that the Spanish settlers would begin devotion to Our Lady of La Leche (Nuestra Senora de La Leche y Buen Parto), Mary nursing the infant Jesus.

In the early 1600s, the Spanish settlers of St. Augustine established the United States' first Shrine to the Blessed Virgin Mary. Now a chapel, pilgrims come from all over the world to pray for Mary's powerful intercession, for fertility, for the health of their children, for safe delivery of those expecting and more. [14]

What we know about our earthly mothers and their devotion to their children is that there is a bond that is everlasting. Jokingly, I have heard it said that a child may let go of their mother's apron strings, but mothers never let go of their child's heart strings. This is true also of my experience with Mother Mary.

I like spending time with her first thing in the morning, waking up, praying the rosary with her for her intentions, as well as for the needs of those around me—my relatives, my friends, my community, the church, and the world. It is a very sweet time early in the morning when I am putting myself and my concerns in her care.

Often people have difficulty in one way or another about praying the rosary, but Scott Hahn in his book *Signs of Life* writes that we should not work hard at praying the rosary, but simply "stop multitasking and abandon ourselves like children to the time we're spending with our mother."[15]

 With the rosary, the Christian people sit at the school of Mary and are led to contemplate the beauty on the face of Christ and to experience the depths of his love. Through the rosary the faithful receive abundant grace, as though from the very hands of the mother of the Redeemer.[16]

It feels better for me to start the day with prayer from the heart, and I receive abundant graces, as Mary forms herself in me. Since she always listens, I can talk to her about many things which are on my heart.

As I meditate on the mysteries of Christ's life through the rosary, whether it is the Glorious, Joyful, Sorrowful, or Luminous, I am also amazed at the closeness to Jesus as well as to Mary.

In *Praying the Rosary Like Never Before*, Edward Sri also acknowledges Jesus as the "center of gravity" of the rosary and writes that every time we say the "Hail Mary," the focus should be on Jesus: he is at the center of the prayer as we speak his holy name. We can all practice this as we pray.

As I recall Jesus' first miracle in the wedding feast of Cana, I think of her as the one who encourages Jesus to "the more" needed in the situation, to produce more wine (John 2:1-11). He listened to her then and he listens to her now.

And that is where we get in touch with the "Queenship"

of Mary. She has such an important role in Jewish history and in the current day. In *Jesus and the Jewish Roots of Mary*, Dr. Brant Pitre explains that another important title and crucial role is as the queen mother. If Jesus is the new Davidic king, then she is the queen mother—as in ancient Israel, it was not the wife of the king who ruled as queen, but the king's mother.

Mary therefore has a special honor. She is there by his side and asks things of him. In Jeremiah 13:18 and Psalm 45, we read that the queen mother reigns with the king. And in 1 Kings 2, we read that the queen mother is royal intercessor.

As a royal intercessor, she can become a prayer warrior, which is what Jeff Cavins pointed out in his Bible study, "Revelation: The Kingdom Yet to Come." [17] He states that the Hebrew name of the queen mother is from the Hebrew root, "gibor" or "warrior." In Hebrew, the queen mother is "Gebirah." So, thinking of God putting Mary in his plan of salvation, I recognize her also as a warrior, an intercessory prayer warrior, which gives me pause to seek her intercession in prayers for urgent protection.

In addition to the rosary, I will pray the *Memorare* [18] when I am in need of a mother's quick response. Weekly, at our church, there is consecration to Our Lady of the Miraculous Medal and the veneration of a first order relic [19] in an Adoration hour. This has particular meaning for me, as we visited the chapel at Rue de Bac France some years ago and I was asked to lector there for the Mass we celebrated–a powerful connection for me to this image of Mary.

† † †

In July 1830, Sister Catherine Laboure in the community of the Daughters of Charity was summoned to her chapel. There, she had a conversation with the Blessed Mother who told her that she was giving Sister Catherine a mission. In the second apparition in November 1830, she saw Mary standing on what seemed like half a globe and the globe was the word, "France." Here there were many troubles in the world. In a third apparition, Sister Catherine saw our Lady standing on a globe with her arms outstretched, and there were rays of light coming out from her fingers. Around the figure were the words: "O Mary conceived without sin, pray for us who have recourse to thee." This prayer supported the dogma of the Catholic church of the Immaculate Conception of Mary (CCC, 491). It also supports my belief in the powerful intercession of this lady who was greeted by the angel "Hail, full of grace" (Luke 1:28).

Clearly, Mary is there in my moments of need and yours; and she teaches us many things, as a mother who loves us— standing by us, as she did in the Passion with Jesus.

One year when I was in spiritual direction school, my daughter had severe dental problems. We were very far from each other physically at the time, however, she continued to send me pictures of her jaw swelling, and I was becoming more concerned with each increasingly horrific picture. I thought of Mary, always with Jesus and in pain at the foot of the cross. Our Lady somehow endured his pain and her own.

In my prayer time, I imagined Mary with me and asked her intercession in our suffering. I sought discernment from her as a mother about a mother's love and action. One of the national speakers at the school, as well as others, were praying for my daughter, but I knew that through the Blessed Mother, spouse of the Holy Spirit, an answer would come to direct my actions. Additionally, I connected to a prayer facilitator at the school, who in praying with me, reminded me of St. Ignatius and his fourteen rules of discernment.

I recognized that I needed to go back to my "original proposals and determinations," Rule number five. [20] And my original proposal was about my love for my daughter and my concern for her being alone in the hospital, where she needed to be for the swelling to be treated.

In spite of my daughter's and others' protests, I applied the rule and immediately made plane reservations. I arrived at the hospital some hours later, carrying our Mother's heart with me to my daughter's bedside. She recovered quickly.

In *Praying the Rosary Like Never Before*, Edward Sri writes that while we may be meditating on the mysteries of Christ's life, we are also entrusting our lives to Mary's intercession when at the end of each decade we say, "Pray for us sinners, now and at the hour of our death."[21]

† † †

In *33 Days to Merciful Love*, Fr. Michael Gaitley comments on John Paul II's description of entrustment. As one takes Mary "into one's own home," this is following Christ's example, as he also entrusted himself to Mary at the Annunciation and through his life that was hidden. Fr. Gaitley wrote that Jesus wants to bring us closer to himself "by giving us to the one who is closest to him, the same one who directs everything to him." At the wedding feast of Cana, she told the servants to do whatever he told them to do.

We entrust our lives in so many ways to Mary so that we can experience her motherly love and to pray for ourselves and loved ones, as mentioned above, and all world intentions. From the messages to the visionary Mirjana on May 2, 2015, the Blessed Mother says:

> I know your pain and suffering because I lived through them. I laugh with you in your joy and I cry with you in your pain. I will never leave you.[22]

Or a further message on Aug. 2, 2014, to Mirjana:

> I am calling you to be my apostles of light who will spread love and mercy through the world. My children,

your life is only a flash in contrast to eternal life.[23]

And as sinners, Mirjana was fond of saying that the Blessed Mother called sinners, "those who don't know the love of God" yet. In the Blessed Mother's apparitions at Fatima in May and October 1917, she directed the children to pray for world peace.

Mary points us toward salvation of souls in the work of Jesus' saving power for peace. Like most people, I am concerned about world peace—peace in our country, and peace in the hearts of men everywhere—so I offer part or sometimes a whole rosary, for renewal of the Church and the peace of Jesus in the world.

The Blessed Mother is a role model for me as mother, a prayer intercessor, and a friend to Jesus. She leads me to follow Jesus in prayer and action. I pray, acknowledging her contemplative spirit and wonderful virtues of humility, gentleness, and grace and ask that she will form me more into the likeness of her and the image of her Son Jesus Christ. She becomes incorporated in me, as an exemplary parent, whom I love and imitate.

In *St. John Paul the Great: His Five Loves*, Jason Evert writes of St. John Paul's *Theology of the Body* and that the gift of self must be free, total, faithful, and life-giving.[24] The highest expression of human freedom is the gift of one's self in love. His devotion to Mary was a total gift to her, but the gift, he writes, was mutual. She gave back the gift of herself.

St. Louis de Montfort writes that when Mary sees someone give him or herself entirely to her, she gives back in a wondrous manner. The person receives abundant graces, and she shares her virtues with the person—her humility, faith, purity, etc. One who is consecrated belongs entirely to Mary, but also Mary belongs entirely to the person.

From the Blessed Mother's message of March 18, 2012 to Mirjana:

> I am coming among you because I desire to be your mother–your intercessor. [25]

I believe that this is the ultimate purpose of our taking Mary into our hearts: so that she can bestow her graces and join us in her mission with Jesus.

From the messages to Mirjana on April 2, 2015:

> I have chosen you, my apostles, because all of you carry something beautiful within you. [26]

Those who say yes are "chosen." Being "chosen" is a gift, and in the next chapter, I will deal more with the steps of consecration and mission.

CHAPTER 9

Prayer, the Blessed Mother,
and the Immaculate Heart

Every once in a while, I run across a person who says that from an early age he or she *knew* he or she was going to be a doctor or a nurse or a journalist, etc. My stepson said he *knew* in fifth or sixth grade that he wanted to attend the Air Force Academy. Years later, this "knowing" was still with him, and he entered and graduated from the Air Force Academy.

On the other hand, as a child, I had little idea what I wanted to "be" in my life vocation, other than a mother. Fleetingly, there were also some silly notions of becoming a celebrity as a singer, or dancer (in that order). I discovered these aspirations listed in an old elementary school picture/autograph book recently.

I only accomplished one of these early goals, and being a mother has to be the best role in life! As for singing and dancing, that is, as they say, "in my dreams." What I like about singing and dancing—not professional choices for me—is that I can do both when I walk or ride my bike around the neighborhood or lead a night of praise and worship at the church. Fortunately, the Lord had other good ideas for my life.

In Jeremiah 29:11-14, we read:

> For I know well the plans I have in mind for you, says
> the Lord, plans for your welfare and not for woe, so as to
> give you a future full or hope. When you call me, and
> come and pray to me, I will listen to you. When you look
> for me, you will find me. Yes, when you seek me with all
> your heart I will let you find me, says the Lord, and I will
> change your lot . . .

I was privileged to become a mother, a very sacred "lot"
in life, after I embraced a career as a Christian clinical social
worker and marriage and family therapist. Continuing to
follow Jesus Christ, I answered the call to become a Third
Order Discalced Carmelite, engaging in a deeper life of
prayer and spiritual commitment. Some years later, I went
through a further transformation of my lot by studying for
and becoming a certified spiritual director. I believe that
these areas of service were part of God's plan for me, initially,
to change my *lot* to work for him.

In Isaiah 43:1 we read:

> But now, thus says the Lord, who created you, Jacob,
> and formed you Israel: Do not fear, for I have redeemed
> you; I have called you by name and you are mine.

When we recognize that we belong to him, we can next accept that he has called us, with a mission in store for us. During Adoration one morning, while attending an annual Carmelite retreat in Alabama, I received a very reassuring message. I heard Jesus say that I *belonged* to him. This was a comforting feeling and gave me permission to let my love for the Lord be even more zealous.

In the New Testament, we are familiar with the story of how the apostle Simon came to be called "Cephas" or Peter by Jesus. In John 1:41-42, we read:

> He first found his own brother Simon and told him, 'We have found the Messiah' (which is translated Anointed). Then he brought him to Jesus. Jesus looked at him, and said, 'You are Simon, the son of John; you will be called Cephas' (which is translated Peter).

Jesus had a mission for Peter, thus a name change for him. In the Word Study about Peter included in *Ignatius Catholic Study Bible, New Testament* (Matthew 16:18), it is stated that there is no evidence that Peter was a proper name before Jesus changed Simon's name to Peter. This indicates the symbolism of the name that Simon is the "rock" and that Jesus builds his church upon the rock. In the Aramaic language, the word *kepha* is the equivalent of Peter and indicates a "sizeable rock," one that is used as a building foundation. The commentator states:

Peter now stands in this biblical transition where new names signify new God-given roles in salvation history. In Peter's case, Jesus designates him the foundation stone of the New Covenant Church....so Jesus builds his NT Church upon the foundational rock of Peter (cf. Eph 2:20; Rev. 21:14).

So, we might ask, "What is God's mission, that may signify his actual name for *us*?" Or, does he want to change our internal and external *lot* or condition?

One thing I have learned well in these years is that there is always "more" with God. In 1 Chronicles 4:9-10 we read:

Jabez was the most distinguished of his brothers. His mother had named him Jabez saying "I bore him with pain." Jabez prayed to the God of Israel: "Oh, that you may truly bless me and extend my boundaries! May your hand be with me and make me free of misfortune, without pain!" And God granted his prayer.

As we go through life, God gives us steps along *his* path for us. Our boundaries can be extended, and whether we pray or not, God will offer us opportunities to move forward with and for him. We can choose.

† † †

A priest I know gives out a bracelet to all that says: "God's got this." He is speaking somewhat to divorced people, encouraging them not to give up with a failed marriage and to believe in a God who promises that "something good will come out of this." The back of Fr. Tony's card reads from Proverbs 3:5-6:

> Trust in the Lord with all your heart and lean not on your own understanding; Acknowledge Him in all your ways, and He will direct your paths.

My work associate and I were once approached by a priest in Panama City who was interested in starting a church project for the homeless. I knew that my heart was not ready to work with "the least of the least," as Fr. Mike was suggesting. I surrendered my heart and the project to the Lord in prayer. "Change my heart O Lord," I sang, and prayed a prayer of surrender.

Soon, I noticed that I was feeling more charitable toward the poor and homeless alcoholics the priest wanted to serve. Together, with several others from the church, we set up a not-for-profit organization and, with a small steering committee of six, we began to fund some programs that became ecumenical, served the poor, and continued in the community for many years.

God can "make lemonade out of lemons." He can turn anything or anybody around for us, that his will is done. He brings about the internal and external changes with little steps for his plan of salvation. A song I love that speaks to this is entitled: "In His Time" by Maranatha. The first and second lines go like this:

In his time, in his time, he makes all things beautiful in his time. Lord please show me every day as you're teaching me your way, that you do just what you say, in your time.

And that is what he does. He teaches us his way and makes us more beautiful. This is occurred in the life of Wayne Weibel, a Myrtle Beach newspaper publisher and columnist. Years ago, I came across his book entitled *Medjugorje: The Message*, published in 1986. Weibel, a Lutheran, learned about the apparitions of the Blessed Mother to six Croatian children in Medjugorje and decided to write an article for his four weekly newspapers.

The story goes that while he was watching a videotape of the apparitions for his research, he felt that the Virgin Mary spoke interiorly to his heart and asked him to write about the events. She said: "You are my son, and I am asking you to do my Son's will. Write about these events and if you choose, the spreading of the messages will become your life's mission." It was not a small step for him, as he was a Lutheran, so for a Lutheran to visit a Catholic village where the Mother of Jesus was appearing was significant!

His life's mission ended up becoming "spreading the messages" of the Blessed Mother in Medjugorje and participating in God's plan of salvation. He traveled with many other pilgrims to this small village in Medjugorje, a total of 129 times over thirty years and wrote twelve books. He died at age 80 in 2019.

Immediately upon my finishing reading his book, *Medjugorje: The Message*, I announced to my associates in the Catholic psychotherapy practice group: "I have to go to Medjugorje. The Blessed Mother is calling." Little did I understand what that meant, but I said yes to her invitation and took the steps she offered. Although we were transformed and experienced miracles there, it would be many years before I clearly realized how this trip was another part of God's mission for me.

† † †

In his book *33 Days to Morning Glory*, Fr. Gaitley features St. Mother Teresa of Calcutta as a teacher of Marian consecration. In 1946 on the train to go to her yearly retreat, he said she experienced a "call within a call" that included visions and mystical experiences.

She felt "the burning thirst of Jesus for love and for souls" and a plea from Jesus to found the Missionaries of Charity

religious congregation. When some time passed, he kept repeating to her "Wilt thou refuse?"[1]

In 1947, she had three visions. In one, she saw the immense sorrow and suffering in faces. When she knelt near
Our Lady, she heard Mary saying: "Take care of them–they
are mine. Bring them to Jesus–carry Jesus to them. Fear not."
In a third vision, the crowd was there again, but lots of darkness. Jesus was on the Cross, Mary a distance away. Teresa
was a little child and in front of the Blessed Mother. Jesus
spoke to Teresa:

> I have asked you. They have asked you, and she, My
> Mother, has asked you. Will you refuse to do this for Me–
> to take care of them, to bring them to Me?[2]

Finally, St. Mother Teresa embraced this call on October
7, 1950. She founded the Missionaries of Charity religious
congregation, an organization to help the extremely poor.

By this story, it seemed that God had asked Mother Teresa to make a conscious decision to dedicate her soul, mind,
heart, and body to God for a higher purpose for him.

A couple of years ago, my husband and I felt strongly the
desire to go to Fatima, where the Blessed Mother had appeared in 1917. What an important Marian visitation, approved by the church; plus, the 100-year anniversary would
be celebrated soon. We were set to go with our local priest

and then decided that the actual time was too short in Fatima. Although we searched widely, we could not find another trip.

In the meantime, someone had given me a book for my birthday entitled *My Heart Will Triumph*, written by Mirjana Soldo, one of the visionaries of Medjugorje. She wrote that Medjugorje was an *extension* of Fatima. We had not heard this interesting connection before. We thought, "If this is true, why not go to Medjugorje to be with her as she related the messages?"

Instead of the trip to Fatima, then, we decided to travel to Medjugorje. We both longed for a deeper relationship with Mary, and to be where she was still appearing seemed an incredible gift.

In our faith journeys, we had both consecrated ourselves to Mary. I had read *True Devotion to Mary* by St. Louis de Montfort many years earlier and had followed the 33-day consecration. This process was rigorous, but worth it. St. Louis de Montfort knew the power of Mary's special role in growth toward God. From his book *The Secret of Mary*, he writes:

Consequently, just as the child draws all its nourishment from the mother, who gives it in proportion to the child's weakness, in like manner do the elect draw all their spiritual nourishment and strength through Mary.[3]

Years later, I consecrated myself again to Mary through the steps with Fr. Michael Gaitley in *33 Days to Morning Glory*. Fr. Gaitley's focus was less on prayers and more on the teachings on Marian consecration through St. Louis de Montfort, St. Maximillian Kolbe, St. Mother Teresa, and St. Pope John Paul II. These teachings were inspiring and life-giving. Perhaps for my personality and the timing of the consecration, the St. Louis de Montfort consecration was significant and necessary.

Finally, my husband and I had prepared for the consecration together through Fr. Hugh Gillespie's book: *Total Consecration to Mary*, and Fr. Gillespie–a Montfort father–brought the spiritual legacy of St. Louis de Montfort's work to modern times.

All of this played a role in our discernment to visit Medjugorje. Three of the six visionaries in Medjugorje were receiving apparitions daily; and in addition, Mirjana received messages on the second of each month and on her birthday. Although there have been numerous apparitions worldwide, only a few of them have been approved by the Catholic Church and, to date, Medjugorje is not one of them. However, you cannot deny the fruit: Reports say more than 19 million pilgrims have visited as of this writing, with countless conversions and lives changed.

To understand how Medjugorje was an "extension" of Fatima, and about how we were living out fully our consecrations and re-consecrations, we had to re-read and pray about the Blessed Mother's messages and appearances in Fatima. Why was she sent by Jesus and what messages did she bring? And what was the connection to Medjugorje? In addition, a significant personal question for us was: Were we living our consecration as fully as Jesus and Mary wanted?

As I mentioned in chapter 2, the Blessed Mother appeared in Fatima, Portugal, from May to October 1917. Pope Benedict XV had called for a novena in honor of Our Lady, the Queen of Peace, since World War I seemed that it would never end. On the eighth day of the novena, May 13, 1917, she made the first of six appearances.

In *Fatima For Today*, Fr. Andrew Apostoli acknowledges how the Blessed Mother appeared in Fatima at a time when mankind had grown forgetful of God and his loving plan of salvation. There was much rebellion to his laws and a selfishness of heart which led to World War I. He wrote:

> In our times of crisis, both personally and as a society, the Virgin Mother of God is always immediately aware of our distress and is always interceding on our behalf before the throne of God. She also faithfully counsels us, with deepest motherly love, to do what Jesus Christ tells us, to turn over our lives to him through prayer and penance.[4]

In addition to the Blessed Mother's appearances in Fat-

ima, 1917, we found much to be learned from visits the children received the year prior. Fr. Apostoli wrote that the Angel of Peace visited the children in 1916 to "prepare the way."
God often prepares his people for the graces and blessings
that will be given them, and there are many instances in the
Old Testament about angels bearing messages.

It seems important to review the revelations of the children as well as the Blessed Mother in teaching us about how
to pray. In the first apparition of the angel in the spring of
1916, the essential message was an invitation to pray; and he
taught the children a prayer, which came to be known as the
"Pardon Prayer" in which the prayer asks God to pardon
those who are not obedient to him.

This became an intercessory prayer for sinners. In the
second apparition, in the summer of 1916, the angel appeared and asked the children to pray and make sacrifices
constantly and make reparation:

> My God, I believe, I adore, I hope, and I love You! I
> ask pardon of You for those who do not believe, do not
> adore, do not hope and do not love You.[5]

Also, the angel said:

> Make of everything you can a sacrifice and offer it to
> God as an act of reparation for the sins by which He is

offended, and in supplication for the conversion of sinners.[6]

Fr. Apostoli writes of the angel's message of Catholic Eucharistic devotion during the third apparition in the Fall of 1916. The angel taught them another prayer to say frequently for reparation:

> Most Holy Trinity, Father, Son and Holy Spirit, I adore you profoundly, and I offer you the most precious Body, Blood, Soul and Divinity of Jesus Christ, present in all the tabernacles of the world, in reparation for the outrages, sacrileges and indifference with which he himself is offended. And through the infinite merits of his most Sacred Heart, and the Immaculate Heart of Mary, I beg of You the conversion of poor sinners.[7]

In the Blessed Mother's first appearance in May 1917, she asked the children if they were willing to offer themselves to God and to suffer as he willed it as an act of reparation for the sins and conversion of sinners. She requested that they pray the rosary daily for world peace.

In her second appearance on June 13, 2017, she made three requests of Lucia–to come back with Francisco and Jacinto on July 13, to pray the rosary every day, and for Lucia to learn to read. The appearances in July and in October were the most important and powerful of all the messages, according to Fr. Apostoli.

In July, she gave serious warnings, but with hope in the victory of her Immaculate Heart. (In October, the miracle promised by Our Lady—the miracle of the sun—was for all to see and verified that the children were telling the truth.)

In her second message in July, her third appearance, she showed the children a vision of hell. This is considered the first of "the three secrets of Fatima." She again encouraged them to pray for the conversion of sinners, and to pray the rosary for lasting peace.

She urged them to put the messages into practice so that souls would be saved, the war would end, and another war—even worse—would not take place, nor famines and other persecutions. Peace had to begin in the hearts of people everywhere, and then that peace could be shared with family and community. She talked about the consecration of Russia to her Immaculate Heart and the Communion of Reparation on First Saturdays.

In July 1917, she promised that she would be victorious:

> In the end, my Immaculate Heart will triumph. The Holy Father will consecrate Russia to me, and she will be converted, and a period of peace will be granted to the world. In Portugal, the dogma of Faith will always be preserved. [8]

She also asked the children to finish a decade of the rosary with a special prayer to save the souls from hell: "Oh my Jesus, forgive us our sins, save us from the fires of hell. Lead all souls to heaven, especially those in most need of Your mercy."[9]

It was on December 10, 1925, in a seventh visitation, that our Lady returned to Lucia only, and asked for a Communion of Reparation and the consecration of Russia to her Immaculate Heart to ward off the terrible tragedies of war, famine, and persecution.

She also requested the "Five First Saturdays" devotion where for five consecutive months one goes to confession, receives Holy Communion, says the rosary, and then meditates for fifteen minutes on the mysteries of the rosary. This practice is done with the intention of reparation to the Immaculate Heart of Mary for the sins and blasphemies by which she is offended.

My husband and I regularly practiced these devotions each month. Yet, in my prayer, I asked Jesus: "Have I truly taken them as seriously as you desire, incorporating them deeply into my heart and lifestyle?" Had my *lot* truly changed from this following of the Blessed Mother's messages? The answers to these questions would surface later.

We planned and went on the pilgrimage to Medjugorje, in spite of the cold, rainy, and wintery weather we had heard about and later encountered. It took three planes and a two-hour bus ride to arrive at the little village of a country that used to be called Yugoslavia and is now an independent piece of it called Bosnia-Herzegovina.

With such feelings of expectancy on both our parts, it was clear to me that the Blessed Mother was calling us. My husband was eager for an "initial" experience, and I yearned for a deepening of that "first love" encounter from the trip with my daughter.

In the village, the Blessed Mother's love and warmth was everywhere, in spite of the cold. We experienced it in the visionaries, in the people of the little village, in the church, and even in the natural environment of fields and hills where we walked.

We were honored to stay at Mirjana's boarding house. Even though still a visionary, she was so humble, loving, and accessible to us. As she literally served us the breakfast and afternoon meals, I felt Mary's joy and motherly love flowing from her. Being in Mirjana's presence felt as if the Blessed Mother was physically with us.

At St. James Church, we attended Mass and Adoration. Just as in my first trip, the villagers seemed remarkable in their reverence of the holy Eucharist in Mass and in Adoration. What I saw was a *lived* faith of the people, practicing the messages to adore and follow Jesus–in prayer, in receiving the Eucharist, in Adoration, praying the rosary daily, and Reconciliation.

Of the nineteen enclosed Reconciliation stations on the outside of the church, I was told there was always a line.

However, since we came in the winter, we were blessed not to wait in a line. The rosary was prayed daily in a crowded church, and one restaurant even made free "fasting" bread, for the Wednesday and Friday fasts, recommended by Our Lady.

For the final interval of our pilgrimage, we traveled to Zagreb for a special meeting with Fr. Jozo, formerly the parish priest in the early years with the visionaries.

In those first days of apparitions, Fr. Jozo did not believe the children, but God used him to protect and hide them from the Communists. At one point, he was thrown into jail for three years for defying the Communist police.

I was so happy to see Fr. Jozo again after my first introduction to him in 1989. Fr. Jozo was still Mary's "apostle of love." He talked about our Lady's messages and then presented us with a postcard of the Blessed Mother, the image we revere as "Our Lady, Queen of Peace."

He blessed the picture and, in a touching part of his presentation, asked us to hold the image over our hearts, praying she would "come into our hearts." I was moved to tears, overwhelmed much like that "first love" of long ago.

On the back of the picture card were her words:

Dear Children, I invite you to individual conversion. This time is for you! Without you, God's plan cannot be implemented. Dear children, grow closer to God day by day through prayer.

Also, on the back of the card, were the messages of the Blessed Mother that lead us to Jesus, which were compiled by Fr. Jozo: Pray the Holy Rosary with the heart, The Eucharist, the Holy Bible, Fasting and Monthly Confession.

Suddenly, I realized again, that God needed us for his plan of salvation, and it was through Mary that we would come into Jesus' vision and purpose. I noticed a new *fire within*, a fresh longing to dedicate myself to her for the mission of Jesus and her mission. I wanted to understand more deeply her messages leading to abundant, sacramental life in the Catholic Church, so that I could bring others to Christ and grow in my faith.

† † †

In *33 Days to Morning Glory*, Fr. Gaitley wrote of John Paul's understanding of a "new motherhood of Mary," which incorporated more love which reached maturity when she was at the foot of the cross and joined in the suffering of Jesus. He remarked that Mary's "new love" changed her so that she "burned" with more love for those for whom Jesus had suffered and died.

And I realized that Mary wants our hearts to "burn" also for those suffering and join in the mission. We heard and saw this as we experienced her visitation in Medjugorje. This meant that our *consecration* also needed an act of *entrustment*.

And what is the idea of *entrustment*? John Paul II in *Redemptoris Mater* wrote that when we, like the disciple John, take her into our homes, we bring her into our human condition; we are seeking her maternal charity. In this way, Jesus brings us closer to himself in sharing with us the one with whom he is closest.

Fr. Gaitley stated:

> This is the whole purpose behind why we entrust ourselves to Mary: It's so she can bring us even closer to Christ through her powerful prayers and motherly love. [10]

Fr. Gaitley wrote that in a *consecration*, God wants us to be involved in the work of salvation to spread the Gospel. He has given various roles to many people and to Mary, he gave a special role: to nurture grace and give birth to Christians that they may "grow to the full stature of Christ." [11]

So, how do we do this? He suggested several prayers, that would indicate a daily *re-consecration*, including a daily rosary and words that indicated that you were giving your life to Jesus daily through Mary. For me, it became the prayer from St. Louis de Montfort's book *The Secret of Mary* as the daily giving of myself to Mary.

After writing *33 Days to Morning Glory,* Fr. Gaitley was

asked why the title, morning glory? He wrote that it is a "new way of life" with Marian consecration.

> The act of consecrating oneself to Jesus through Mary marks the beginning of a gloriously new day, a new dawn, a brand-new morning in one's spiritual journey. It's a fresh start, and it changes everything. [12]

My husband and I felt she was calling us into a new deeply *lived* consecration. We discovered the beauty of a daily *re-consecration* that St. Louis de Montfort encouraged.

In *Total Consecration to Mary*, Fr. Hugh Gillespie stated that St. Louis de Montfort recommended *daily re-consecration* in a simple manner, with the goal of deepening and renewing an attentiveness to a *total belonging* to Mary. He reiterated that St Louis de Montfort wrote not only of consecration but also of *re-consecration*. Consecration was not simply words of gestures of the moment, but:

> ...a fundamental movement of self-giving and self-surrender, an act of radical belonging to the Lord through Our Lady, that asserts itself in every aspect of life. Every gesture, every thought, every decision, every concrete action, however great or small it may be, is given into the hands of Mary for the glory of Almighty God. [13]

I believe that this is an important step, and one that my husband and I practice. St. Louis de Montfort wrote that the prayer could be simple and authentic. Fr. Hugh Gillespie gave the following example:

> I am all yours, and all that I have is yours, O my dear Jesus, through Mary, your Holy Mother. [14]

We awakened to fasting anew, as the Blessed Mother requested fasting on Wednesdays and Fridays. Making the sacrifices with food fit with the messages from the Angel of Peace in Fatima when he taught the children to make little sacrifices often to save sinners. Fasting off food and drink was one way to save sinners.

In her extended interview with our group of pilgrims, Mirjana also explained that fasting leads to more prayer, which often prompts one to seek Reconciliation, where the heart is then cleansed. Praying with the heart is spoken of frequently in Medjugorje. In the preface of his book *Pray With the Heart: Medjugorje Manual of Prayer*, Fr. Slavko Barbaric, O.F.M. writes:

> When you come to Medjugorje, you will hear that we are called to prayer, not only to the one in the morning or evening, to the individual or common prayer, but to the prayer with the heart as well. [15]

The process of fasting, prayer, confession, and cleansing the heart was becoming clearer. As I fast and pray, I am also discovering attachments to material or physical comforts, as well as spiritual comforts[16] which may not be in the Lord's plan for me.

As I confess those, my heart becomes humble and pure. Fasting, though difficult, would bring me into more of the Lord's plan and his will for me. My husband found fasting easier than I, and he was a model for me.

From Our Lady's message to Mirjana on January 2, 2014:

> Dear children, for you to be able to be my apostles and to be able to help all those who are in darkness to come to know the light of the love of my Son, you must have pure and humble hearts...[17]

Purifying my heart and entrusting my heart and my life to Jesus through Mary seemed urgent—not just for my conversion, but also to spread her messages to help lead others out of that darkness.

St. John of the Cross, one of my favorite Carmelite saints, is known for his writings on detachment. In his book *Fire Within*, Fr. Thomas Dubay described how John held that anyone who is serious about loving God *totally* must not involve himself with "self-centered pursuit of finite things sought for themselves, that is devoid of honest direction to God, our sole end and purpose."[18]

Conversion through the Heart of Mary was such a central message of Fatima, as well as Medjugorje. It is worth repeating, lest it appear insignificant or get lost: For our hearts to become connected to the Blessed Mother's heart is essential in God's plan of salvation.

In the book *Fatima: A Message More Urgent Than Ever*, Luiz Sergio Solimeo writes that the Blessed Mother appeared to the visionaries in Fatima on June 13, 1917 (the second apparition). It was the feast day of Saint Anthony. She said:

> Jesus wants to establish devotion to my Immaculate Heart in the world. That Immaculate Heart will be the 'refuge' of pious souls and a safe path to salvation, the way that leads to God. [19]

Solimeo writes further that the whole theology of devotion to Our Lady and to her Immaculate Heart is understood that it is Jesus who is laying the foundation for devotion to His Mother's triumph and who has established a way back to God. It is his plan that we go to him through Mary Most Holy. [20]

Fr. Gaitley wrote that St. Mother Teresa of Calcutta believed that when we give our hearts to Mary, there is a kind of exchange of hearts: We give Mary our hearts, and she gives us her Immaculate Heart. For St. Mother Teresa this gift through consecration is expressed in two prayers: "Lend me your heart" and "Keep me in your most pure heart." [21]

To St. Mother Teresa, "Lending the heart" means that she is asking Mary to help her to love with the perfect love of her Immaculate Heart, so that she can live out her vocation. It is through the Holy Spirit, who is indwelling, that the Immaculate Heart is bonded with the Holy Spirit. As Maximillian Kolbe wrote: "The Holy Spirit does not act except through the Immaculata, his spouse."[22]

The second prayer is: "Keep me in your most pure heart." Fr. Gaitley writes that Saint Mother Teresa is asking for Mary's heart to be in her, and for her to be in Mary's heart. He writes: "So this is a prayer to love Jesus through Mary, in Mary, and with Mary."[23]

If we lend our hearts to Mary, we are asking for Mary's heart to be in us and for us to be in Mary's heart. And we are seeking the power of the Holy Spirit for our hearts to be bonded with Mary's heart and to keep our hearts pure, like hers.

In 1992, Pope John Paul II offered a new understanding of consecration as dying for another and "consecrating his life to the Immaculate Virgin," in the way that St. Maximilian Kolbe had done. St. John Paul then endorsed the Kolbean example (1917) of Marian *consecration* as a critical element of the *"new Evangelization"* for the third Christian millennium and St. Maximilian as a primary intercessor. Prayer is the main weapon in the spiritual battle with evil, he said.

And consider this message to Mirjana from Our Lady on August 2, 2014:

I am calling you to be my apostles of light who will spread love and mercy through the world. My children your life is only a blink in contrast to eternal life. [24]

In teaching a *Total Consecration to Mary* class, I find that people are hungry to know the Blessed Mother. Lay people are taking time to work on consecration—to be involved in God's plan of salvation.

Mirjana continues to write that the Blessed Mother wants us to join the fight on earth by helping our brothers and sisters come to know God's love. Our Lady said, "I desire that, through love, our hearts may triumph together." [25]

Will you be a part of the triumph of Her Immaculate Heart by accepting her into your heart and allowing your life to be transformed in love? We are asking for Mary's heart to be in us; and for us to be in Mary's heart. We are setting ourselves aside for God through Mary. And setting apart means consecration. Fr. Gaitley wrote that as we entrust ourselves to Mary's prayers, she will intercede for us so that we can give ourselves to Jesus' divine heart in his work of redemption.

Perhaps her mission to intercede for us is stated best in the words of St. Pope John Paul II on the occasion of his visit to rue de Bac, Paris, France in 1980:

Blessed are you among women! You are intimately associated with the work of our Redemption, associated with the Cross of our Savior; your heart has been pierced, next to His heart. And now, in the glory of your Son, you never cease to intercede for us poor sinners.

In the third part of his consecration prayer, St. Maximilian Kolbe stated:

> If it pleases you, use all that I am and have without reserve, wholly to accomplish what was said of you: 'She will crush your head, and, You alone have destroyed all heresies in the whole world.' Let me be a fit instrument in your immaculate and merciful hands for introducing and increasing your glory to the maximum in all the many strayed and indifferent souls, and thus help extend as far as possible the blessed kingdom of the most Sacred Heart of Jesus. [26]

Through all of these experiences, including our Medjugorje pilgrimage, I've learned that not knowing what I was to become when I grew up had its advantages. By allowing myself to see where God leads next and following the lead of Mary's Immaculate Heart, new evangelism can follow.

In the next chapter, we'll see how our consecration to the Immaculate Heart leads us into experiencing more of the Lord's Divine Mercy.

CHAPTER 10

Divine Mercy and Prayer

In my first class at the Cenacle Spiritual Direction School in Clearwater, Florida, Dr. Ron Novotny, Co-Director of the Cenacle, asked: "Did you know that God is crazy about you?"

This question simultaneously overwhelmed and thrilled me! In fact, it's so profound that I am still trying to take it in more than a decade later. My prayer is that, through this chapter, you will come to realize and experience the magnitude of the question and the truth of God's unfathomable love and bottomless mercy just for you.

Growing up Protestant, the two biggest things I believed about God were: I knew he was faithful and that *our* faithfulness mattered to him, and I knew that God was not *about* love, but that God *was* love. These two ideas about faithfulness and love of God were anchors in my soul and faith walk. And after reading numerous spiritual works and growing in my understanding of him, they are still my foundation.

However, these roots have grown even deeper; as I gain more knowledge, I continue to personally experience God's *merciful love.*

In elementary school, I recall standing at an outdoor water fountain and fiddling with a mustard seed necklace on my neck. It contained a real, tiny mustard seed enclosed in a piece of plastic with a silver seal, and I never took it off. I may have even worn it to bed. It hung on my neck like a short set of pearls, and to me it was just as valuable.

Of course, I had memorized the scripture in one of my Presbyterian Sunday school classes:

> …If you have faith the size of a mustard seed, you will say to this mountain, 'Move from here to there,' and it will move. Nothing will be impossible for you (Matthew 17: 20-21).

In my first chapter, I recounted an experience I had in a second grade Sunday school class. The memory has stayed with me, as it was significant in my journey with God. One Sunday morning our teacher, "Miss Betty," taught us to embroider on a small piece of red cloth, with white thread, a bookmark that read: "God is love."

I still remember what Miss Betty looked like as well as the classroom of that church. I have a photo of her in one of my childhood scrapbooks and still have that bookmark, tucked between the pages of my favorite bible.

After all these years of witnessing others' experiences with God, and pondering my own, I know that the bookmark could be "re-embroidered" with a more accurate description. Instead of "God *is* love," I re-imagine the bookmark to say, "God is *merciful* love."

This understanding of *God's merciful love* wasn't in my vocabulary as a youngster growing up in the Presbyterian Church. This is no reflection on that church or any denomination. God's timing for me to understand more would come through the Catholic Church. As I look back, I see so many instances intellectually, as well as experientially, of a merciful, loving God.

In his 1988 theological retreat for the contemplative community, "Handmaids of the Precious Blood," Fr. John Hardon talked about "The attributes of God." He wrote that God, in his infinite wisdom, has a will; and in that will, he loves his creatures (us) and practices "Infinite goodness."[1]

I asked myself, *What is infinite goodness?* Somehow it seems easier to think of "God as love" on an intellectual level, but to recall *how* God loves us in those everyday experiences of our lives is the *infinite goodness* part that feels so right.

Fr. John explained that creation is a manifestation of *divine love.* God did not have to create the world; and this is evidence of his *goodness.* The human race had no claim on God's love because it rejected it. But when mankind (Adam and Eve) sinned—rejecting the advances of his infinite love—God decided to still love man.

Then God showed *mercy* when he redeemed the world through Jesus Christ. God does not have to love us after we have committed grievous sins; he does not *owe* us anything. And yet he *chooses* to love us, so much that his only son became man and died for our sins.

Another attribute of God that Fr. John talked about is his *ongoing mercy* that flows from *infinite goodness*. When we sin, we lose all claim to his love, *except* through the blood of Jesus Christ. And yet, he, out of his *infinite goodness*, does not withdraw from us.

In *The Second Greatest Story Ever Told*, Fr. Michael Gaitley writes about God's mercy and describes a fifteen-year journey of discovering God in a new way. He came to understand that God's ways are not our ways, and he doesn't love as we love—which may be because someone is attractive, funny, talented, rich, or powerful. Fr. Gaitley writes:

> He loves us because we need his love. He loves us because he's good, not because we are. He loves us because his heart is full of *merciful love*, the kind of love that, like water, rushes to the lowest place.[2]

This is so comforting to me—knowing that God does not withdraw from us. In my youth, I needed his *infinite goodness,* and needed him to pour out his *merciful love* many times: to rush to my lowest place—and he did. In my desperation, I encountered his *merciful love,* without completely understanding the magnitude of the gift given until later. And I am still learning!

† † †

As a child, after my father was elected to Congress, we began our yearly moves to Washington for half the year while Congress was in session (January to June). I was in the fifth grade, so I went to an elementary school at home in South Carolina half the year and one in the Washington, D.C., area for the other half.

By the time I reached the seventh grade and academic studies became more complex, my parents decided to send me to St. Agnes Episcopal School for Girls in Alexandria, Virginia—boarding the first part of the school year, then living with my parents when they arrived.

Boarding school was difficult for me in those three years as I was homesick for my family and friends. I was teased by my much more worldly roommates from other parts of the country. On the top bunk of four bunk beds in that dorm room, I often cried at night under my covers. I was in a very *low place*. Scripture captures that feeling for me:

> Gracious is the Lord and just; yes, our God is merciful. The Lord keeps the little ones; I was brought low, and he saved me (Psalm 116:5-6). [NAB St. Joseph edition, 1970]

Although I could recite numerous scriptures about God's mercy as a youth, I could not truly "name" it yet. God's mercy is everywhere in scripture, in both the Old and New Testaments.

Father God had *mercy* on the Israelites as he brought them to the "Promised Land," and he repeatedly forgave their disobedience and continued with them on their journey to the Promised Land (a good video series on this is Jeff Cavins' *Salvation History*).

In the New Testament Gospel of John, we read:

All things came to be through him, and without him nothing came to be. What came to be through him was life, and this life was the light of the human race; the light shines in the darkness, and the darkness has not overcome it (John 1:3-5).

And later in that same chapter, we are told:

And the Word became flesh and made his dwelling among us, and we saw his glory as of the Father's only Son, full of grace and truth (John 1: 14).

In Jesus—"the Word made flesh"—God gave us a physical example of his *merciful love*. From the beginning of Jesus' public ministry, as recorded in the New Testament, we read of the miracles and healings of Jesus: the multiplication of the fishes and the loaves, Jesus Christ in his Passion, Resurrection and Ascension to free us, to heal us, to save us from our sins.

† † †

One time at the boarding school, I was quarantined with an infection and stayed in the school infirmary for two weeks. I was by myself, except for visits from the nurse. It was very lonely, and emotionally difficult for me, with no visitors allowed. Even though my mother wrote me a little white postcard every day, I was in a very *low* place. Yet, even then I knew that, though physically alone, God was with me, and I was not truly alone. God in his *mercy* kept me company.

In *The Second Greatest Story Ever Told*, Fr. Gaitley writes that *mercy* becomes love when it is confronted with poverty, weakness, brokenness, and sin. This kind of love has power to bring "good out of such evil."[3] Fr. Gaitley says that God gives *mercy* when we need it most. "In the darkest era, we need the brightest light to keep us from giving up and losing heart."[4]

Weekends were often the most difficult at the boarding school. I recall intensive wailing one Saturday when I was quite homesick and feeling desperate for a friend—someone to talk to—but I didn't know anyone who could listen to my pain. I rushed to a classroom in the school, where I knew I could be alone with God and openly cry and express myself.

I recall wailing, seeking God, and knowing somehow in his infinite goodness and *mercy,* he would listen to me. I knew, unlike anyone else, he would comfort and befriend me. My wailing stopped; and I felt consoled. And in this moment, at the early age of thirteen, I learned experientially that Jesus could be trusted. As Fr. Don, pastor of St. John the Evangelist Church in Panama City, used to say: "Jesus showed up." So, in my distress, in my misery, in those excruciating moments, there came a touch from Jesus that brought *balance* to the emotional turmoil within me.

This touch signaled a deeper healing and blessing, not only emotionally and spiritually for this one time, but for all times. And I discovered the mercy of Jesus, from his infinite goodness, though I could not "name" it yet. He was there for me in my lowest place.

I believe it was in this encounter that my relationship with Jesus Christ was solidified internally; you might say that a bond was established, deeply embedded. It I became part of me, though out of my awareness.

I could trust him to "show up," in more abundance than I could ask for or imagine. He would meet me exactly where I needed, then, but again and again, as needed.

I think back to that first night at the Cenacle Spiritual Direction School when Dr. Ron Novotny remarked: "Did you know that God is crazy about you?" I was filled with tears. It reminds me now of the Gospel scripture, Luke 7: 36-40 of the woman who wept and wet Jesus' feet with her tears and dried Jesus' feet with her hair in her gratefulness to him.

And it wasn't until much later that I understood the concepts of Divine Mercy and trust in Jesus, which are so beautiful and sustaining, through his apostle of Divine Mercy, Sister Maria Faustina Kowalski.

Sister Faustina in her *Diary* wrote a prayer imploring Divine Mercy, titled *God's Love is the Flower - Mercy the Fruit.* It begins:

"Let the doubting soul read these considerations on Divine Mercy and become trusting." One of the lines is "Divine Mercy, lifting us out of every misery, I trust in you."[5]

A reflection on this poem, published by The Marian Fathers, states:

Mercy is where God meets us in our misery. He loves us in our misery, in our brokenness, and so wants to lift us out of our misery into his very Heart. Every pain, every sin, every place where you feel you are inadequate or too broken, God loves. He loves you in every area of your life that you believe you could never be loved.

He wants to forgive every sin. He wants to heal every wound. He wants to comfort and console every sorrow. Trust in him. He will never abandon you. Trust in him. He will never leave you in your misery. He will lift you up and set you on high. Call upon him and he will be with you in times of distress.[6]

In reading St. Faustina's poem and the reflection which the Marian Fathers offered, I particularly appreciate the idea that God comes to us in our misery. How many times have we called upon him in distress and found that he sends people our way to meet us and direct us to his *mercy*?

† † †

After several days of pain and inability to eat properly, we sought help at a recommended nearby medical clinic. I was diagnosed with an infection on a stone that I had had for a while in my parotid gland on the right side. I was first prescribed a medicine that had no effect on the infection. And consequently, I could not eat or sleep because of increasing pain and discomfort. I was trying diligently to hide my difficulty as I did not want to be a "bother" to our friends.

My husband and I and another couple once vacationed on the Island of Oahu in Hawaii. This was their first time in Hawaii, and it was important to me that their experiences somehow matched ours: complete relaxation and awe of the beauty of the plants and foliage, as well as the friendliness and good will of the Hawaiian people. On the first day, I had trouble eating on one side of my mouth. At a nearby clinic, I was diagnosed with an infection on a stone in the parotid gland. I was prescribed a medicine that did not work. I could not eat or sleep because of the pain and I was trying diligently not to be a bother to the other couple, as it was their first time in Hawaii.

Several instances of a merciful and healing Jesus followed. Returning to the same clinic, I was assigned another physician who prescribed the correct medicine. How deeply grateful was I for this physician, who had treated the condition before. Calling Mayo Clinic in Jacksonville for an appointment then, I was surprised when told that I needed a CT scan or there was no appointment. I called the physician at the clinic, and, in his kindness, he immediately arranged a CT scan at the hospital, minutes before we were to leave for the airport to return to Panama City, where we lived then. After the scan, I picked up the disc, and we boarded the plane, with an appointment set at Mayo, for the day after we returned.

The God-arranged events continued. The Mayo ENT physician diagnosed my condition as warranting a procedure called "saliendoscopy." This was still a new and rare procedure in the U.S. It required specialized training, which this ENT doc didn't feel qualified to perform. He referred me to two specialists, somewhat in my geographical area, one of whom was completely "booked up" and was one of the trainers in the U.S. Although I would have preferred to see him, I set an appointment with the other physician at the University of Alabama. In the meantime, I had a "raging" infection, which necessitated I remain on another round of the antibiotics until I could have the procedure (as stated to me by a retired physician who was a good friend).

Worried that I could not locate a physician who would go with this protocol, again in my lowest place, I found a physician's assistant (P.A.) at a nearby clinic in Panama City Beach, who took my word for it and was willing to prescribe the exact antibiotic with the correct prescription strength. He made a mistake at first, prescribing a lesser strength. When the notice came from the physician in Alabama about the confirmed appointment, he also made a mistake about the appointment date.

I saw this as a "sign" and "took a chance" and called the trainer at the University of South Carolina Medical College in Charleston, South Carolina. The receptionist told me that he would be at a conference on the dates that I needed. Within a day, while seeing clients in my psychotherapy office, my husband alerted me that this ENT physician, Dr. Marion Gillespie, planned to get in touch in a few minutes. Very apologetically, I excused myself.

Dr. Gillespie wanted to take the case. He explained he would be coming back from a conference in Canada but could be there to perform this surgery. I tried to let him "off the hook," commenting, "I don't want to put pressure on you. Won't you be tired?" But he insisted. He said: "I like the pressure. I will see you then." I had the surgery at the scheduled time in that October 2013, and he became a friend for

life. I found out that he was a strong Christian, participating
on mission trips. He understood the movement of God in
our lives.

I believe that God, in his Divine mercy, arranged this appointment. Dr. Gillespie said that the surgery, lasting four
hours, had turned out to be more complicated than he
thought. I often wondered after this if I had had the surgery
with the other physician, would it have worked out so well?
Would he have been skilled enough for this more complicated, new procedure?

God in his mercy is the Divine Physician and directed
my course. The greater good out of this difficult time seemed
for me to appreciate and trust in Jesus' care. And then, my
sister, who had suffered with the stone in the parotid gland
for many years, being mis-diagnosed and advised not to have
any surgery, decided to" take a chance also." She was quite
pleased; and we referred others to this ENT surgeon. I often
say now that God has saved my life many times through the
doctors he has directed me to and empowered.

One of the first books I read on the topic of mercy was
by Fr. John Hampsch, *The Awesome Mercy of God*. The late
Fr. Hampsch tells us:

> The world's worst sinner can be forgiven in a fraction
> of a second by simply saying to the Lord, with true sin-
> cerity, 'I'm sorry.' No matter what our situation—

whether we are feeling burdened by sin, enduring temptation, coping with illness, or struggling with doubt—God's healing love is as near as the air we breathe.[7]

As beautiful as this is, do we trust that "God's healing love is as near as the air we breathe"? And that he is ready to forgive and heal us—to have mercy on us?

In *The Second Greatest Story Ever Told,* Fr. Michael Gaitley writes that we still don't trust God, which is a leftover from our first parents, Adam and Eve. He says that trust is restored in the Blessed Mother as the "new Eve" and Jesus as the "new Adam."

Fr. Gaitley often uses the phrase: "God's School of Trust." He writes that God wants us to trust in his *merciful love,* and in the physical manifestation of this love is his Son, Jesus Christ.

What I have gathered from the extensive work of Fr. Gaitley, however, is that we first need to understand fully that the *merciful heart* of Jesus also has the other dimension of sorrow, a *sorrowful heart.* The former was revealed by Jesus to St. Faustina and the latter by Jesus to Sister (now Saint) Margaret Mary. And this sorrowful heart is in need of our consolation.

Fr. Gaitley's book *Consoling the Heart of Jesus* helps us understand that Jesus wants us to acknowledge his Sacred Heart, covered with thorns and wounded for lack of love, needing consolation.[8]

Jesus showed this clearly to a French cloistered Margaret Mary Alacoque in the 17th century. In a series of three visions in 1663, he showed her his heart, full of love, and he explained that his Sacred Heart needed consolations for the offenses and sacrileges against it. He appeared on the Cross and said:

> Behold this heart that so deeply loves mankind, that it spared no means of proof—wearing itself out until it was utterly spent. This meets with scant appreciation from most of them; all I get back is ingratitude—witness their irreverence, their sacrileges, their coldness and contempt for me in this Sacrament of Love.[9]

Jesus wanted Sister Margaret Mary to spread his love, yet he asked as well for *reparation* on the First Fridays for nine consecutive months.

Assisted by her confessor, Fr. (now Saint) Claude de la Colombiere, Sister Margaret Mary said that Jesus called for the establishment of a feast in honor of the Sacred Heart and for prayers for the *reparation* for sins, especially those directed against the Eucharist.[10]

In *Fatima for Today: The Urgent Marian Message of Hope,* Fr. Andrew Apostoli explains *reparation*:

> ...an act of love to God to help make up for someone's failure or refusal to love him. In other words, when a person offers some good deed or act of self denial as

reparation to God, he is saying, 'God, I love you' in order to make up for an offense against him by which someone else said 'God, I do not love you.'[11]

If we review more recent history in the Blessed Mother's early 20th century apparitions at Fatima, we understand that in the summer of 1916, the Angel of Peace taught the three visionaries a prayer of *reparation* they were to recite three times. It's called the "Pardon Prayer," which I detailed in Chapter 9.[12]

As mentioned in that last chapter, the angel urged them to pray for the salvation of souls and "to make of everything you can a *sacrifice.*"[13] In a third appearance in later September or early October, the Angel of Peace taught the children to pray a prayer of *reparation* for offenses against the Eucharist three times, also.

These prayers of *reparation* are more meaningful for me every day as I become aware of the many ways that I, personally, and others offend God daily, through distractions during Mass or irreverence at Communion or during Adoration. I strive to pray these prayers of *reparation* several times daily.

Fr. Gaitley points out that although Jesus is "happy" in heaven and may seem no longer to suffer, he needs consoling. His book *Consoling the Heart of Jesus* explains *retroactive consolation* by looking at Pope Pius XI's encyclical letter, *Miserentissimus Redemptor,* who seems to endorse the idea of *retroactive consolation*; although he does not use the phrase. Fr. Gaitley quotes a paragraph from this letter:

...we can and ought to *console* that Most Sacred Heart which is continually wounded by the sins of thankless men ... [14]

A theologian of the Sacred Heart, Timothy O' Donnell S.T.D., commented on this encyclical that Jesus did see us and, although he was sorrowful for our sins, he also received *consolation* with our actions of love.

Just as [Jesus] allowed himself to be saddened by the vision of the sins of mankind, so did he also allow himself to be *consoled* by all the human acts of compassionate *consolation* through history until the end of time. So, despite the fact that the future consolers of our Lord were not personally present during the passion, the reparatory value of their foreknown actions did in fact *console* Christ. This loving *consolation* was received by our Lord not in an ever-growing sequence, but instantaneously in his *nuns stans*—everlasting now. [15]

We can *console* Jesus by our works of mercy, both corporal and spiritual (*CCC*, 2447). For instance, we can provide shelter and food for the poor and homeless, we can visit the prisoners, we can instruct the faithful, we can forgive and bear wrongs patiently, etc.

And we can also *console* him through the Nine First Fridays *devotion* that he specified. Through Sister Margaret Mary, he asked that we receive communion in honor of his Sacred Heart on nine consecutive first Fridays of the month.

† † †

Our church has traditionally offered a First Friday Mass with all night public Adoration beginning at 8:00 P.M. and ending with benediction at 8:00 A.M. the next morning. My husband and I practice these First Friday devotions.

In response to another popular devotion in the early 20th century, we also honor the Blessed Mother through the Five First Saturdays devotion. Our Lady made this request as a way to make reparation for the offenses against her Immaculate Heart. This devotion was given to the children of Fatima in the June 13 and July 13, 1917, apparitions.

She told the children that she would return to ask for the consecration of Russia to her Immaculate Heart and the *Communion of Reparation* on the First Saturdays. In a private apparition to the remaining seer, Sister Lucia, years later, she explained what she wanted in "the Communion of Reparation" and the consecration of Russia to her Immaculate Heart to prevent war, famine, and persecution.[16]

On Dec. 10, 1925, the Blessed Mother appeared to her in Pontevedra, Spain. Sister Lucia recorded the experience in the third person, as requested by her spiritual director. She recalled that she was shown the Virgin with the Christ Child and he said:

> Have compassion on the Heart of your most holy Mother covered with thorns, with which ungrateful men pierce it at every moment, and there is no one to make an act of reparation to remove them.

Then the most holy Virgin said: "Look, my daughter, at my Heart, surrounded with thorns with which ungrateful men pierce me at every moment by their blasphemies and ingratitude. You are least trying to console me and say that I promise to assist at the hour of death, with the graces necessary for salvation, all those who, on the first Saturday of five consecutive months shall confess [their sins], receive Holy Communion, recite five decades of the rosary, and keep my company for fifteen minutes while meditating on the fifteen mysteries of the rosary, with the intention of making *reparation* to me."[17]

So, in response to these requests, on the First Fridays of the month, my husband and I attend Mass to receive holy communion and spend time in adoration as a means of consoling the Sacred Heart of Jesus and making reparation for past and present offenses against his love. We also make sure we've examined our conscience and made an act of contrition if we haven't or cannot receive the sacrament of Reconciliation within ten days of the devotion (before or after). And on the first Saturdays, we attend Mass to receive holy communion, pray a rosary and spend fifteen minutes with Our Lady, meditating on the fifteen mysteries of the rosary to make reparation for offenses against her Immaculate Heart.

As for the bigger picture, Fr. Michael Gaitley in *The Second Greatest Story Ever Told* wrote that the consecration of Russia was not completed until March 25, 1984, and was done by Pope John Paul II at St. Peter's Square. The Pope said:

> Let there be revealed, once more, in the history of the world the infinite saving power of the redemption: the power of *merciful Love!* May it put a stop to evil! May it transform consciences! May your Immaculate Heart reveal for all the *light of hope.*[18]

The pope understood the importance of what the Blessed Mother was asking with *consecration* to her Immaculate Heart. He also made the *connection* between the *reparation* to the Sacred Heart of Jesus and the Immaculate Heart of Mary, as well as the Divine Mercy, a devotion that came closer to the middle of the 20th century.

† † †

When Jesus appeared to Sister (now Saint) Faustina in Poland, beginning in the early 1930s, he came with an image of his *merciful* Heart, an image of Divine Mercy, from the cross. In her *Diary*, St. Faustina heard the words inside of her:

> "These two rays issued forth from the very depths of My tender mercy when My agonized Heart was opened by a lance on the Cross. These rays shield souls from the wrath of My Father. Happy is the one who will dwell in their shelter, for the just hand of God shall not lay hold of him" (Diary, 299).

He also told her:

> "Paint an image according to the pattern you see, with the signature: 'Jesus, I trust in You. I desire that this image be venerated, first in your chapel, and then throughout the world" (Diary, 47)." [19]

Jesus says of the image:

> [This image] is to be a reminder of the demands of My mercy, because even the strongest faith is of no avail without works. [20]

Interesting to me is the word "demand" of his mercy and the messages of trust in God and the practice of love of neighbor.

In *33 Days to Morning Glory,* Fr. Gaitley said Pope John Paul II indicated that with consecration and entrustment to the Blessed Mother and the Immaculate Heart, she would lead us to "the fount of mercy," Jesus' Divine Mercy. The pope also stated that consecration to the Immaculate Heart of Mary meant drawing near, through the Mother's intercession, to the "Fountain of Life that sprang from Golgotha," the pierced side of Christ. And he further explained that consecration means "returning to the Cross of the Son."[21]

So, "returning to the Cross" is significant as we see how Jesus leads us through Sister Faustina Kowalski to his *merciful heart,* on the cross and an image of Divine Mercy, with not the thorns, covering the heart, as in the Sacred Heart image, but with rays of red and white flowing out coming from his heart, one hand on his heart and another raised, detailed earlier.

From *St. Faustina's Diary,* we learn that for four years, 1934 – 1938, Sister Faustina was instructed by Jesus to keep a journal of her talks with him. He talked to her about his merciful heart and wanted her to spread his message. Below are a few examples. He said:

> You are the secretary of My mercy; I have chosen you for that office in this and in the next life.

...to make known to souls the great mercy that I have for them and to exhort them to trust in the bottomless depth of My mercy.

...Before the Day of justice, I am sending the Day of Mercy.[22]

In *The Second Greatest Story Ever Told*, Fr. Gaitley wrote that Pope John Paul II, from the earliest moments of his priesthood into his position as pope, understood and revealed his insights in the famous last meditative chapter of his encyclical *Dives in Misericordia* when he wrote of "...the importance of calling out for God's mercy even with loud cries."[23] He remarked further that the church was in great need for mercy.

And we know that as we entered the 21st century, he established a Great Jubilee Year of the Incarnation 2000, the Year of Mercy. And on the second Sunday of Easter, Divine Mercy Sunday, he canonized St. Faustina as the first saint of the new millennium. He ended his homily by calling St. Faustina a "gift for our times."[24]

Fr. Gaitley re-stated again in *The Second Greatest Story Ever Told* that it is the Immaculate Heart that wants to lead us to Divine Mercy. Mary always points us to Jesus.

In my faith walk, it is Mary, in her mystical way, who leads me to keep the *Diary* by my bedside for nightly reading. And opening a page and reading about his merciful love can be compared to opening a treasure chest with jewels falling out. I can feel his merciful presence in every dialogue with Sister Faustina. I am led to appreciate more fully as St. Paul states in Ephesians 3:18-19:

> ... may have strength to comprehend with all the holy ones what is the breadth and length and height and depth, and to know the love of Christ that surpasses knowledge, so that you may be filled with all the fullness of God.

And at the 3:00 hour, particularly in the afternoons, but anytime, we can glorify him in his Divine Mercy by praying the Divine Mercy chaplet. Recently, a friend told me that she awoke at 3:00 a.m. and prayed the chaplet for a friend who had an infection.

Through the chaplet, which I pray daily, I can beg for mercy for groups of persons saying: "Eternal Father, I offer you the body and blood, soul and divinity of your dearly beloved Son, our Lord Jesus Christ, in atonement for our sins and those of the whole world," [25] and "O blood and water which gushed forth from the heart of Jesus as a fount of mercy for us, I trust in you!" [26]

We can pray each day for one of the groups of persons in the novena given to Sister Faustina by Jesus according to the Divine Mercy Institute. [27] Every group seems to be included: those who are sinners, priests and religious, devout and faithful souls, those who do not believe in God and those

who do not yet know Jesus, souls who have separated themselves from the Church, the meek and humble and souls of
little children, souls who venerate and glorify His mercy,
souls who are detained in purgatory, and those who are lukewarm.

We are seeking reparation, but also asking mercy for
them and for ourselves.

And of Divine Mercy Sunday, the second Sunday of
Easter, an extraordinary time of *mercy*, Jesus said:

> I want this image . . . to be solemnly blessed on the
> first Sunday after Easter; that Sunday is to be the Feast of
> Mercy.[28]

> I desire that the Feast of Mercy be a refuge and shelter
> for all souls, and especially for poor sinners.[29]

> …whoever approaches the Fount of Life on this day
> will be granted complete remission of sins and punish-
> ment.[30]

In *The Second Greatest Story Ever Told,* Fr. Gaitley said
Pope John Paul II declared we are now in "the time of
mercy." Sister Faustina prophesied that this is a "new splendor" in the church.

> There will come a time when this work, which God

is demanding very much will act with great power, which will give evidence of its authenticity. It will be a new splendor for the Church.[31]

When Pope John Paul II dedicated the Shrine of Divine Mercy on August 17, 2002, at the conclusion of his homily, he included an act of entrustment of the whole world to Divine Mercy:

How greatly today's world needs God's mercy!...

Today, therefore, in this Shrine, I wish *solemnly to entrust the world to Divine Mercy*. I do so with the burning desire that the message of God's merciful love, proclaimed here through Saint Faustina, *may be made known to all the peoples of the earth* and fill their hearts with hope. May this message radiate from this place to our beloved homeland and throughout the world. May the binding promise of the Lord Jesus be fulfilled: from here, there must go forth 'the spark which will prepare the world for his final coming' (*Diary*, 1732).[32]

Afterword

In this final segment of *The Call to Prayer: Intimate Moments with God*, I'd like to offer a few words about "the call," at this particular moment in history.

In his book *Thirsting for Prayer*, Fr. Jacques Phillipe states:

> What the world most needs today is prayer. It is prayer that will give birth to all the renewals, healings, deep and fruitful transformations we all want for society today. This world of ours is very sick, and only contact with heaven will be able to cure it. The most useful thing for the church to do today is to give people a thirst for prayer and teach them to pray.[1]

With the pandemic of 2020 still with us, although not as widespread as before (praise God for his mercy), the worldwide threat and spread of Totalitarianism, most recently in Ukraine, and—in the United States—the mounting rise of secularism and humanism, the changing politics from a pro-life administration into a "culture of death," plus concerns about immigration, religious freedom, the disintegration of the family and family values, there is much to seriously consider. As we face these challenges, there seems even more of an urgent need to *go big* with our prayers. I call it the *now* call to prayer.

What is the *now* call to prayer? During these last few years and particularly in this time of the pandemic, we must ask ourselves, "How is the Holy Spirit leading and teaching us?"

Again, in the words of Fr. Philippe, "This world of ours is very sick, and only contact with heaven will be able to cure it."

In *The Second Greatest Story Ever Told*, Fr. Michael Gaitley, writes:

> Now is a time of great, extraordinary, and unprecedented grace and mercy for the Church and the world. Now is a time when God is making it easier than ever to become saints. Now is the "end time" when, by calling out for mercy, we can prepare the world for the Lord's final coming.[2]

As mentioned in the previous chapter, if Fr. Phillipe is correct and "this world of ours is very sick and only contact with heaven will be able to cure it," I ask: "Lord, what and how do you want me to pray *now* for "the cure" that will "prepare the world for the Lord's final coming"?

✝ ✝ ✝

I related in chapter 2 about seeing my father kneel at the foot of his bed to pray as I was on the way to the kitchen for breakfast in the morning. I am not sure what he prayed for or how long he stayed there, but one thing was certain: He was seeking God. This was a wonderful image for me as a young girl.

On Sunday mornings, my father awoke early, and I would see him in the dining room (his make-shift study) with Bibles and concordances, taking notes on a triple-fold legal pad yellow page. He was preparing for his 9:00 Sunday School Men's Bible class teaching at the Presbyterian church.

I never asked, but I feel certain that he must have preceded the Bible study with much prayer to develop that day's lesson or subject matter. Looking back as an adult, I now wonder if he had a personal and trusting relationship with Jesus or knew about his merciful love.

I am the type of person who asks plenty of questions now, but growing up, we were not encouraged to ask such things. I now wish I had asked my dad lots of questions, particularly about his spiritual life. *Who was God to him?* and *What did he talk to God about in those early mornings? What were the lessons he taught to the men on Sunday mornings? Did he know Jesus personally and trust him?*

What meaningful and intimate conversations these might have been. And, perhaps as he shared with me about this merciful loving God, I would have said, "Dad, teach me to pray."

† † †

All forms of prayer to which we are called, including those mentioned in this book, are good and essential. All have purpose in fulfilling God's plan of salvation—whether we are on our knees when we first wake up, sitting in our favorite easy chair praying through scripture, or seeking God's will as we move throughout the day. I love that God gives us so many avenues to connect with him and opens the doors widely for us to be *intimate* with him. Intimacy can mean talking to him and listening to him about our own individual and family needs or wider and bigger prayer.

It seems considerable intimate and intercessional prayer is needed now with the global pandemic taking a toll on our families, church communities, and relationships. Our monthly virtual prayer group sought the Lord specifically related to our concerns for the world. We asked, "Lord, how do you want us to pray?"

As the pandemic started in 2020, there was much suffering and fear, with live-stream-only Mass, daily and on weekends. In our prayer group, we sensed that the Holy Spirit wanted us to pray rosaries—many rosaries—in intercession. Perhaps a prophetic word from Our Lady of Fatima?

To follow the Holy Spirit's leading, we asked our pastor and received permission to gather outside for bi-weekly rosaries. We wore face coverings and practiced social distancing, as we interceded through the Blessed Mother on behalf of many intentions, including an end to the COVID-19 virus, protection for healthcare providers, and for a vaccine and for healing.

† † †

There had been a call to intercession in the early days of the pandemic. On April 22, 2020, while serving as the president of the United States Conference of Catholic Bishops, Los Angeles Archbishop José Horacio Gómez sent a letter to all American bishops inviting them to join him in reconsecrating the United States to the Blessed Virgin Mary in response to the pandemic. This reconsecration was under the title of "Mary, Mother of the Church" and took place May 1, the same day bishops in Canada reconsecrated their country under the same title. His letter stated, "This year, we seek the assistance of Our Lady all the more earnestly as we face together the effects of the global pandemic."[3]

In addition, thousands of Christians gathered for a prayer march in Washington, DC on Saturday, September 26, 2020, for deep and widespread intercession. "The Return" was organized by Evangelist Franklin Graham and author Jonathan Cahn. It was based on the scripture 2 Chronicles 7:14:

…if then my people, upon whom my name has been pronounced, humble themselves and pray, and seek my face and turn from their evil ways, I will hear them from heaven and pardon their sins and heal their land.

Many groups of prayer intercessors gathered that same morning off-site, including our church group. During that time, we experienced a call to repentance, and intercession. The highlight of the morning for me was a priest's witness about our Blessed Mother in the image of Our Lady of Guadalupe, and her inspiration in his priesthood. A lay person also talked about the "touch" of Mary in healing. It was a time of humbling and expectant faith and hope.

Although the need seems more urgent now, humbling ourselves and seeking God is not a one-time situation. If I can see myself as "creature" rather than a self-reliant "creator," I can be more pliable to his will instead of my own.

So, what is he asking us to do as we humble ourselves? I think he is asking us to pay attention to the leading of Jesus, the Holy Spirit, and the Blessed Mother. The Holy Spirit is our advocate and leads us to truth (John 15:26), and the Blessed Mother provides maternal mediation, protection. She teaches us how to pray, warns us to avoid calamities, and moves us to the sorrowful and merciful heart of Jesus where we will be saved.

We know that she urges our connection to Jesus—with both his sorrowful and merciful heart—through repentance, reparation, the rosary, prayers and sacrifices for sinners, our country and world peace. According to Janice Connell in *Meetings with Mary: Visions of the Blessed Mother,* she states:

> The Mother of Jesus is the Eternal Mother who brings light, strength, hope, and guidance from God to His precious children of the earth. She alone brings Christ through the divine power of the Holy Spirit, as she did at the Incarnation (Luke 1: 34-36). By her cooperation with the will of God, Mary is the spouse of the Holy Spirit. Those who draw near her draw near the Holy Spirit of eternal love. [4]

If we humble ourselves…and allow ourselves to see what God is doing.…we realize that we have all the information and guidance we need to take action in the *now* call to prayer.

† † †

We have been given many indications on what the "now" call to prayer might look like. To review: Sister Margaret Mary in 1663 of France was visited by Jesus who gave her the First Nine Fridays devotion for reparation and consolation of his Sacred Heart for the offenses against it and the Feast of the Sacred Heart. In 1917, the children of Fatima were visited by the Blessed Mother who taught them prayers and reparation for sinners, to pray many rosaries for world peace, and that her Immaculate Heart would triumph. Through honoring the five First Saturdays with reparation and consolation for offenses against her Immaculate Heart, calamities could be avoided. Jesus visited Sister Faustina in 1931 in Poland and showed her his merciful heart and gave her instructions for how to honor Divine Mercy with the Feast of Divine Mercy on the second Sunday after Easter, the Chaplet of Divine Mercy, and the Novena of Divine Mercy.

In Pope John Paul II's homily in Fatima on May 13, 1982, he said the whole meaning of the Marian and Divine Mercy consecrations is "to allow Mary to bring us to the pierced side of Jesus, the 'Fountain of Mercy.'" And, the Pope, now Saint, stated that consecration to the Immaculate Heart of Mary meant "drawing near through the Mother's intercession, to the very heart of Golgotha."[5]

In his *Explaining the Faith Series: Understanding Divine Mercy*,[6] Fr. Chris Alar, a Marian Father of the Immaculate Conception, states that Jesus said to Sister Faustina, "Mankind will not have peace until it turns with trust to My Mercy (*Diary*, 300)."

In *The Second Greatest Story Ever Told*, Fr. Gaitley writes that Sister Lucia specifically asked Jesus why consecration of Russia to Mary's Immaculate Heart was so important and he told her:

Because I want my whole Church to acknowledge

that consecration as a triumph of the Immaculate Heart of Mary, in order to later extend its [following] and to place devotion to this Immaculate Heart alongside devotion to my Sacred Heart.[7]

So, our first step may be to make the *intentional* decision to get to know the Blessed Mother on a deep and personal level. Beyond quickly praying many rosaries, are we praying to her from the heart? Do we have a personal relationship with her as "mother," so that we seek her and listen to her? We may start with understanding her through praying the rosary as a "head" task and then ask for our hearts to be transformed so that we experience the warmth of her friendship.

Have we made an act of consecration to her? And do we renew it every day?

In one of his YouTube videos, Fr. Chris Alar insisted we are not doing enough of First Fridays and First Saturdays. We should see Mary as commander-in-chief. She is calling us to the Gospel, repentance, and holiness. He states: "Her [Mary's] orders are first Fridays and first Saturdays." Fr. Chris teaches extensively about the First Friday and the First Saturday devotions, so that "the Lord's hand will not strike." Again, these devotions lead us to Divine Mercy and Divine Mercy saves souls.

He explained that these devotions are in *reparation*, which I elaborated on more in Chapter 10, for the sins against the Sacred Heart of Jesus and the Immaculate Heart of Mary. He encourages us to pray, as the power of prayer can change any chastisements.

In short: prayer works, and prayer can change the seemingly most impossible things. Isn't that what Divine Mercy is all about? "Jesus, I trust in you." With God's Divine Mercy at work, not only a good, but a *greater* good can come out of evil. That is, if we pray faithfully as the Blessed Mother and Jesus have taught us.

† † †

That is exactly what happened in Pope John Paul II's life. You may recall the vision that Sister Lucia had of a bishop dressed in white being killed; and then the later attempted assassination of Pope John Paul II on May 13, 1981—the anniversary of the first appearance of the Blessed Mother in Fatima. The bullet that was perfectly aimed to kill our beloved Pope did not; his life was spared. It is clear that prayer changed this outcome. As Pope John Paul II said about his survival: "One hand fired, and another guided the bullet."[8]

As stated in *The Second Greatest Story Ever Told, Fr. Gaitley* points out that the Pope did not die because of "the power of freedom, Our Lady, and Divine Mercy."[9] Fr. Gaitley explained that his life was given back perhaps because of the rosaries, penances, and First Five Saturdays devotions encouraged by the messages of Our Lady of Fatima. To me, that statement is significant and attests to the power of prayer.

Add to that what Cardinal Ratzinger, Pope Benedict XVI, said about the incident related it to our human freedom. He said that the fact that Pope John Paul survived:

> ...only shows once more that there is no immutable destiny, that faith and prayer are forces that can influence history, and that, in the end, prayer is more powerful than bullets, and faith more powerful than armies."[10]

Let that last line sink in. "… prayer is more powerful than bullets, and faith more powerful than armies." It is such a strong statement, and in my mind it's *believable*.

Although I didn't have a chance to ask my dad how to pray, I like to think that he believed that prayer could change things and that prayer and God's mercy can overthrow the greatest obstacle and bring about a great good. I know I do!

It is a time for all of us to get on our knees, just as I saw my dad do, and continue the above devotions and practices ....from our hearts.

And we even have a greater advantage. Because my father was not Catholic, he didn't know about the rosary, making sacrifices for sinners, praying reparation, and bringing consolation to the Sacred Heart of Jesus and the Immaculate

Heart of Mary through our First Friday and First Saturday devotions. He also did not know of a Sister Faustina of Poland who was Jesus' secretary of Divine Mercy.

When I think about all we've been given, I am grateful. And I'm humbled that Jesus, the Holy Spirit, and the Blessed Mother have taught me and *called* me to prayer; and that I can share with others how Jesus and Mary want us to pray, so that we can join in to "prepare the world for the Lord's coming."

My prayer for you is that after reading this book: *The Call to Prayer: Intimate Moments with God,* you are led to "thirst for prayer," to pray deeply, and ask questions of God. That you truly ask yourself, "What does he want of me in his *now* call to prayer?" And "How can I help?"

Always recall Matthew 7:7, "Ask and it will be given to you; seek and you will find; knock and the door will be opened."

What's next for you? Will you ask? Will you seek? Will you say: "Lord, teach me to pray" and let that door open wider and deeper?

I end with a prayer based on words Jesus himself gave to the great "secretary" of Divine Mercy, Faustina: May the binding promise of the Lord Jesus be fulfilled: From here, there must go forth "the spark which will prepare the world for his final coming."[11]

Acknowledgments

The development of this book has been a lengthy process, with most of it concentrated in the last five years. I continue to be grateful to the Holy Family and Holy Spirit for the call, and the inspiration, to write *this* particular book.

I could have never imagined the fruit that would come as a result of my question to Fr. Ted Sosnowski, pastor of St. Bernadette Catholic Church, in Panama City, Florida. The content is a result of his answer and "yes" for my teaching a course entitled: "The Call to Prayer." Thank you, Fr. Ted, for trusting me not to mislead your flock.

I appreciate my parents, Bob and Isabelle, who loved me the best they could and modeled for me "prayer in action" in their caring for others and through their good works in the community and in the state.

An early mentor who taught me about the importance and meaning of prayer and God's love is my long-time friend and associate in psychotherapy practice, Flo Bilelo, a clinical social worker. From her devotion to prayer and the Catholic Church, she encouraged my entry into a Catholic/ecumenical prayer group and later joining the Catholic Church. She introduced me to the Association of Christian Therapists, whose charism is prayer, and the 3rd order Discalced Carmelite order with charisms of meditative and contemplative prayer. She accepted me into The Cornerstone, a Catholic psychotherapy practice group. Thank you, Flo, for these innumerable gifts, but, most of all, for loving me unconditionally through my faith walk, as my spiritual friend and mentor.

I am grateful to the rest of my clinical associates: Lyman, Rick, Carol, Denise, Gloria, Cathy, and Catie who engaged with me in the learning process of how to work appropriately in the spiritual dimension of prayer with clients.

Truly, all of these relationships informed and transformed my prayer life. I learned about the Blessed Mother, St. Joseph, the saints, the holy angels, and the power of the Holy Spirit, and Jesus as healer of body and soul.

I am also appreciative of all that I learned and experienced about prayer in the clinical professions through my friends in the Association of Christian Therapists, particularly Fr. Lou Lussier, O.S. Cam., M.D., Ph.D.; Fr, Bob Sears, S.J., Ph.D.; the late Barbara Shlemon Ryan, R.N., Fr. Richard McAlear, O.M.I., Doug Shoeninger, Ph.D., Fr. Paul Feider, Dr. Len Sperry, Diane Brown, Foundress of the Cenacle and ACT leader, and ACT members and Directors of the Cenacle: Adrienne Novotny, M.A., and the late Ron Novotny, Ph.D. and many others. And a big thank you to my current pastor, Monsignor Keith Brennan, who allowed me, as a spiritual director, to present Advent and Lenten retreats which focused on prayer, and to practice spiritual direction.

I am grateful to all my children and family members, for

my cousin, Peyton who insisted, and encouraged me, that I was genetically-wired to write, as my father was a writer. I want to acknowledge my stepdaughter, Liz, who consistently encouraged me with her optimism to talk about my book, when I wanted to keep quiet.

To my daughter, Heather, who has such rich inner expression of the spiritual world. Through her insights, I have been helped to see what I could not see alone. And to all those trusting souls, who have taken my classes on aspects of prayers, participated in retreats in which I have presented and my spiritual directs: Thank you.

In support of this book, I am most grateful to Julie Bettinger, my developmental editor, who understood how to move me to a greater inner depth and excellence in writing. In her modeling, guidance, devout Catholic identity and spirituality, Jesus was shining brightly and leading.

A special note of gratitude to Dr. Mahfood at En Route Books and Media, LLC, for his appropriate and timely affirmations, as well as his gentle approach, and spiritual wisdom in the details of publication of this book. Thank you.

And, finally, to my husband, Augie, who loves me enough to want the best for me and to be the best for God. He realized early on that I needed understanding and encouragement, and he gave that to me boundlessly, which helped me to grow and flourish in putting my ideas on paper. I love you.

Special Note Concerning the Back Cover

Special note concerning the back cover art drawn from the website of The National Shrine of Our Lady of La Leche (https://missionandshrine.org/about-us/our-story/):

General Pedro Menéndez de Aviles, sent by King Phillip II, arrived at the coast called "La Florida" from Spain in September 1565. His men arrived in hopes of establishing a colony, securing the land for Spain, and most importantly converting the Native American Indians to Christianity. Father Francisco Lopez de Mendoza Grajales wrote in his diary:

"On Saturday [September] the eighth the General landed with many banners spread, to the sounds of trumpets and the salutes of artillery. As I had gone ashore the evening before, I took a cross and went to meet him, singing the hymn 'Te Deum Laudamus.' The General, followed by all who accompanied him, marched up to the cross, knelt and kissed it. A large number of Indians watched these proceedings and imitated all that they saw done."

The website explains that "[f]ollowing Father Menéndez's veneration of the Cross, thus proclaiming this Land in the name of God (Nombre de Dios) Father Lopez celebrated

Mass at a rustic altar made of wood. The sky served as the roof for what was the first parish Mass in what is now the United States. It was on this sacred ground that the Spanish settlers would begin devotion to Our Lady of La Leche, Nuestra Señora de La Leche y Buen Parto, Mary nursing the infant Jesus. In the early 1600's, the Spanish settlers of St. Augustine established the first shrine to the Blessed Virgin Mary in the United States."

A beautiful shrine, restored many times, reflects the devotion of the citizens of St. Augustine. On October 10, there was the placement of a newly-crowned image of Our Lady of La Leche in the chapter. The new image depicts the Virgin Mary nursing the infant Jesus. The Cross was erected in 1965 to celebrate the city's 400th birthday. This gleaming stainless steel cross is 208 feet in height, the tallest free-standing cross in the Western Hemisphere, and marks the location where the Spaniards came ashore to proclaim the site of St. Augustine in the Name of God, Nombre de Dios.

About the Author

Forrest Hemphill Yanke, D.PHIL., LCSW, LMFT

Forrest Hemphill Yanke is a retired licensed clinical social worker and a licensed marriage and family therapist who
has integrated her Catholic faith and knowledge of Christian
healing into her therapy and teaching practices. For 35 years,
she maintained a private practice in Christian psychotherapy
in Panama City, Florida, where she was also instrumental in
developing an intensive case management program for the
homeless. As a result of her teamwork in homelessness, she
was awarded the Jefferson Award for Public Service in Panama City and selected to compete nationally in Washington
D.C.

She taught Pastoral Counseling and Called and Gifted
courses as an instructor for the Institute of Ministry Formation after formation for the Diocese of Pensacola-Tallahassee and was as an adjunct professor in the College of Social Work at Florida State University, Panama City campus.

For over 25 years, she served as a psychological expert
witness for the Catholic Marriage Tribunal in the Diocese of
Pensacola-Tallahassee and has been recognized throughout
her career with many awards for her professional work.

Dr. Forrest Yanke earned a doctorate in Religion and Societal Studies from Oxford Graduate School and holds a certificate in Spiritual Direction through the University of Steubenville and the Cenacle of Our Lady of Divine Providence House of Prayer in Clearwater, Florida. She is a professed member of the Secular Order of Carmelites and a long-time member and former president of ACTHEALS.

Currently, she serves as outreach coordinator for the separated and divorced at her church and teaches classes on prayer and healing. She currently serves as a Stephen Minister in her church and co-facilitates Living Waters Prayer Ministry.

Forrest is married to August Yanke, and they have four children between them and seven grandchildren. They reside in Ponte Vedra Beach, Florida.

Endnotes

Chapter 1

[1] St. Teresa of Avila, *The Autobiography of St. Teresa of Avila: the Life of St. Teresa of Jesus Written by Herself* (Rockford, IL: Tan Books and Publishers Inc., 1997), Para. 7.

[2] Fr. Jacques Philippe, *Thirsting for Prayer* (New Rochelle, NY: Scepter Publishers, 2014), 12.

[3] Max Lucado, *Before Amen: The Power of a Simple Prayer* (Nashville, TN: Thomas Nelson, 2014), 9.

[4] "Laying on of hands." The *Catechism of the Catholic Church* states that "Holy Baptism is the basis of the whole Christian life, the gateway to life in the Spirit, and the door which ties access to the other sacraments" (CCC# 1213). For the sacrament of Confirmation, the baptized are "enriched with a special strength of the Holy Spirit" (CCC# 1285). So the Holy Spirit was given to me in the sacraments of Baptism and Confirmation, with the laying on of hands. In his book *The Power of Healing Prayer: Overcoming Emotional and Psychological Blocks* (Our Sunday Visitor Publishing Division, Huntington Indiana, 2012), Fr. Richard McAlear, OMI, defines "touch" as the second principle of healing, as he quotes from the Scriptures about "the laying on of hands." Fr. McAlear writes that over half of the healings of Jesus occurred with some kind of touch and in the Gospel of Mark, he sent out the apostles and instructed that those upon whom hands were laid

would recover (Mark 16:18). Fr. McAlear further states, "The laying on of hands is a gesture that is interwoven in the very life of the church" (38). "Touch is important in healing prayer because it conveys a human connection as well as the love that is the Spirit of God" (38).

[5] From *Christian Anthropology: The Nature of the Human Person, Human Brokenness, and Healing*, Unit III, ed. by Douglas Schoeninger, Kenneth Fung, Robin Caccese, Louis Lussier, Bonita Lay (McLean, VA: The Association of Christian Therapists, 2009), 159.

[6] Ibid., 169.

[7] Thomas Dubay, *Prayer Primer: Igniting a Fire Within* (San Francisco, CA: Ignatius Press, 2002), 25.

[8] Ruth Burrows, O.C.D., *Essence of Prayer* (Mahwah, NJ: HiddenSpring), 28.

[9] Fr. Larry Richards, *Surrender: The Life-Changing Power of Doing God's Will* (Huntington, IN: Our Sunday Visitor), 27.

[10] Ibid., 26.

[11] Jason Evert, *Saint John Paul the Great: His Five Loves* (San Francisco: Ignatius Press, 2014), 134.

[12] Ibid., 134.

[13] Conrad De Meester (translated by Salvatore Sciurba) *Brother Lawrence of the Resurrection: Writings and Conversations on the Practice of the Presence of God* (Washington, DC: ICS Publications, Institute of Carmelite Studies, 1994), 114.

[14] Ibid., 105.

[15] Ralph Martin, *Fulfillment of all Desire: A Guidebook for the Journey to God Based on the Wisdom of the Saints* (Steubenville, OH: Emmaus Road Publishing, 2006), 300.

[16] Evert, *Saint John Paul the Great,* 129.

[17] Ibid.

[18] Ibid., 130.

[19] Fr. Jacques Philippe, *Time for God* (New York, NY: Scepter Publishers, Inc., 1992), 10.

[20] Pope Benedict XVI, *A School of Prayer: The Saints Show Us How to Pray* (San Francisco, CA: Ignatius Press, 2013), 9.

[21] Thomas Dubay, *Prayer Primer: Igniting a Fire Within* (San Francisco, CA: Ignatius Press, 2002), 19.

Chapter 2

[1] Fr. Chad A. Ripperger, *Deliverance Prayers: For Use by the Laity* (Denver, CO: Sensus Traditionis Press, 2020), 9.

[2] Fr. John Horgan, *His Angels at Our Side* (Irondale, AL: EWTN Publishing, Inc.2018), 270.

[3] Lisa Brenninkmeyer. *Fearless and Free: Experiencing Healing and Wholeness in Christ Bible Study.* For reference, visit online: https://shop.walkingwithpurpose.com/products/fearless-and-free

[4] Bob Schuchts, Ph.D. Lecture "Prayer for Inner Healing," *Healing the Whole Person Conference*, Tallahassee, Florida, March 14, 2017.

[5] Lisa Brenninkmeyer. *Fearless and Free: Experiencing Healing and Wholeness in Christ Bible Study, 177.* https://shop.walking-withpurpose.com/products/fearless-and-free

[6] Overview of Carmelite Practices. St. Albert of Jerusalem is revered by Carmelites as he honored the holiness of hermits who lived on Mount Carmel about the year 1200. The Brothers of the Most Blessed Virgin of Mount Carmel asked Albert for a written

formula of life by which they might live in obedience to Jesus, which he provided to them between the years of 1206–1214. This document was approved by Pope Innocent IV in 1247 and is still essential to the Carmelite family in the twenty-first century. It has a sound scriptural foundation. Following are the principles of the Rule: Living in allegiance to Jesus Christ; being diligent in meditating on the law of the Lord; giving time to spiritual reading, participation in the church's liturgy–both the Eucharist and the Liturgy of the Hours; being concerned for the needs and the good of others and the community; practicing virtues and living in faith, hope, and charity; seeking interior silence and solitude in the life of prayer; and using prudent discretion in all actions.

Further, the origin of the Discalced Carmel is found in St. Teresa of Jesus (Avila). Her teachings on prayer and the spiritual life are foundational in the formation and life of the Secular Order. Known as St. Teresa of Jesus, she made prayer an important part of one's whole life in a search for union with God. Prayer is to be nourished by God's word and personal contemplation to "nourish their mission in the world," so that they can be true witnesses in the world. For a fuller understanding, read *The Book of Documents of the Washington Province of the Discalced Carmelite Secular Order*, Washington D.C., 2018, pages 9-43.

[7] Ralph Martin, *The Fulfillment of All Desire*, annotated edition (Steubenville, OH: Emmaus Road Publishing, 2006), 37.

[8] Ibid., 37. St. Francis of Sales, Introduction to the Devout Life (Pantianos Classics, Original, 1609), 37.

[9] Dan Burke, *Into the Deep: Finding Peace Through Prayer* (North Palm Beach: Beacon Publishing, 2016), 3.

[10] Consecration: Many books cover consecration to the

Blessed Mother, including *33 Days to Morning Glory*, by Michael E. Gaitley and *Preparation for Total Consecration to Jesus through Mary*, by Fr. Hugh Gillespie. I personally used prayers from *The Secret of Mary* by St. Louis De Montfort. And for my more recent consecration to St. Joseph, I used prayers from *Consecration to St. Joseph: The Wonders of Our Spiritual Father*, by Fr. Donald Calloway.

[11] Ripperger, *Deliverance Prayers*, 18.

[12] *Christian Prayer: The Liturgy of the Hours* (New York: Catholic Book Publishing Co., 1976), 7-8

[13] Scott Hahn, *Signs of Life: 40 Catholic Customs and Their Biblical Roots* (New York: Doubleday Religion, 2009), 229.

[14] Pope Benedict XVI, *A School of Prayer: The Saints Show us How to Pray* (San Francisco: Ignatius Press, 2016), pp. 33-39.

[15] EWTN devotionals. https://www.ewtn.com/catholicism/devotions/morning-prayer-written-by-st-therese-838

[16] Fr. Andrew Apostoli, CFR, *Taken From Fatima for Today: The Urgent Message of Hope* (Ignatius Press, San Francisco, 2010), 23 and 35.

[17] Angel of Peace Fatima Prayers: The two prayers that the Angel of Peace taught the children to pray (three times each) are the Pardon Prayer: "My God, I believe, I adore, I hope, and I love You! I ask pardon of you for those who do not believe, do not adore, do not hope and do not love you…" and the reparation prayer: "Most Holy Trinity, Father, Son and Holy Spirit, I adore you profoundly, and I offer you the most precious Body, Blood, Soul and Divinity of Jesus Christ, present in all the tabernacles of the world, in reparation for the outrages, sacrileges and indifference with which he himself is offended. And through the infinite merits of his most

Sacred Heart, and the Immaculate Heart of Mary, I beg of You the conversion of poor sinners.

[18] Fr. Slavko Barbaric, O.F.M., *Pray with the Heart! Medjugorje Manual of Prayer* (Franciscan University Press, 1988), 9.

[19] *Chalice of Strength, Prayers for Priests: Crusade of Prayer and Reparation for Priests* (Opus Sanctorum Angelorum), 24.

[20] *Eucharist Adoration for the Sanctification of Priests and Spiritual Maternity* (Congregation for the Clergy, 2007), 24.

[21] Archives Du Carmel de Lisieux (accessed July 2, 2021), Letter 94: https://www.archives-carmel-lisieux.fr/english/carmel/index.php/lt-91-a-100/1101-lt-94-a-celine

[22] https://aletiaorg/2017/when-padre-pio-was-visited-by-a soul-from-purgatory/

[23] https://www.ourcatholicprayers.com/prayers-for-souls-in-purgatory.html

[24] *Catechism of the Catholic Church,* second edition (Washington, D.C.: U.S. Catholic Conference, Inc.), Glossary "Real Presence," 896.

[25] Vinny Flynn, *7 Secrets of the Eucharist.* (Stockbridge, Massachusetts: MercySong Inc., 2006), 7.

[26] Ibid., 10.

[27] Ibid., 11.

[28] https://catholicmasses.org/public-mass-ban-in-italy-leads-to-new-focus-on-spiritual-communion/

[29] St. Maria Faustina Kowalska, *Diary of St. Maria Faustina Kowalska: Divine Mercy in My Soul* (Stockbridge, MA : Marian Press, 2012), *Notebook* II, paragraph 914.

Chapter 3

[1] Jacques Gauthier, *I Thirst: Saint Therese of Lisieux and Mother Teresa of Calcutta* (Alba House, 2005), 26.

[2] Fr. Timothy M. Gallagher, O.M.V., *The Discernment of Spirits: An Ignatian Guide for Everyday Living* (New York: The Crossroad Publishing Company, 2005), 13-14.

[3] Fr. Marc Foley, O.C.D., *The Dark Night: Psychological Experience and Spiritual Reality* (Washington, D.C.: ICS Publications, 2018), 16.

[4] Ibid., 14.

[5] Fr. Marc Foley, O.C.D. (translated from the original manuscript by John Clarke), *Story of a Soul: The Autobiography of Saint Therese of Lisieux, A Study Edition* (Washington, DC: ICS Publications, Institute of Carmelite Studies, 1996 third edition; Study Edition 2005, 2016), 316.

[6] Ibid., 317.

[7] Ibid., 305.

[8] Fr. Jacques Phillipe. *Time for God* (New York: Scepter Publishers, Inc. 2008), 15.

[9] Fr. Jacques Phillipe, *Interior Freedom* (New York: Scepter Publishers, Inc. 2007), 64.

[10] Fr. Richard McAlear, OMI, *The Power of Healing Prayer: Overcoming Emotional and Psychological Blocks* (Huntington, IN: Our Sunday Visitor, 2012), 74.

[11] Fr. Richard McAlear, OMI, *Forgiveness: Experiencing God's Mercy, New and Expanded Edition* (Self published, 2017), 19.

[12] Jack Canfield, Mark Victor Hansen, Patty Aubery, Nancy Mitchell, *Chicken Soup for the Christian Soul: 101 Stories* (Deerfield Beach, FL: Health Communications, Inc., 1997), 4.

[13] Phillipe, *Interior Freedom*, 56.

[14] Ibid., 54.

[15] Mother Teresa, *No Greater Love* (Novoto, CA: New World Library, 2001), 20.

Chapter 4

[1] Infused contemplation is "An infused supernatural gift that originates completely outside of our will or ability, by which a person becomes freely absorbed in God producing a real awareness, desire, and love for him. This often gentle or delightful and sometimes non-sensible encounter can yield special insights into things of the spirit and results in a deeper and tangible desire to love God and neighbors in thought, word, and deed." As described in the spiritual dictionary of terms, Dan Burke with Fr. John Bartunek, *Navigating the Interior Life: Spiritual Direction and the Journey to God* (Steubenville, OH: Emmaus Publishing, 2012), 127.

[2] Cardinal Robert Sarah, *The Power of Silence: Against the Dictatorship of Noise* (San Francisco, CA: Ignatius Press, 2017), 57.

[3] Fr. John A. Hardon, S.J., *Catechism on the Real Presence* (Bardstown, KY: Eternal Life, 1998), 58.

[4] Fr. Sean Davidson, *Saint Mary Magdalene: Prophetess of Eucharistic Love* (San Francisco: Ignatius Press, 2017), *as reviewed by Tom Perna: https://tomperna.org/2018/07/21/saint-mary-magdalene-prophetess-of-eucharistic-love/*

[5] Linda Schubert, *Miracle Hour: A Method of Prayer That Will Change Your Life* (Santa Clara, CA: Miracles of the Heart Ministries, 1993).

[6] Ibid., 3.

[7] Fr. Michael E. Gaitley, MIC, *Consoling the Heart of Jesus: A Do-It-Yourself Retreat* (Stockbridge, MA: Marian Press, 2011), 45.

[8] Robert Cardinal Sarah, with Nicolas Diat, *The Power of Silence: Against the Dictatorship of Noise* (San Francisco: Ignatius Press, 2017), 22.

[9] Ibid., 58.

[10] Jacques Gauthier (translated by Alexandra Plettenberg-Serban), *I thirst: Saint Therese of Lisieux and Mother Teresa of Calcutta: A Striking Commonality in the Spiritual Foundation of Saint Therese of Lisieux and Blessed Mother Teresa of Calcutta* (Staten Island, NY: St. Paul's, 2005), 154.

[11] St. Maria Faustina Kowalska, *Diary of St. Maria Faustina Kowalska: Divine Mercy in My Soul* (Stockbridge, MA: Marian Press, 2012) *Notebook* VI, paragraph 1717.

Chapter 5

[1] Fr. Larry Richards. CD: *Confession* (Lighthouse Talks Augustine Institute).

[2] St. Maria Faustina Kowalska, *Diary of St. Maria Faustina Kowalska: Divine Mercy in My Soul* (Stockbridge, MA: Marian Press, 2012) *Notebook* VI, paragraph 1602.

[3] Vinny Flynn, *The 7 Secrets of Confession* (Stockbridge, MA: MercySong, 2013), 70-71.

[4] Scott Hahn, *Lord Have Mercy: The Healing Power of Confession* (New York, NY: Doubleday, 2003), 146.

[5] Flynn, *The 7 Secrets of Confession*, 27.

[6] Richards. CD: *Confession.*

[7] Kowalska, *Diary of St. Maria Faustina Kowalska, Notebook* VI, paragraph 1725.

[8] Fr. Paul Farren. *Freedom and Forgiveness: A Fresh Look at the Sacrament of Reconciliation* (Brewster, Massachusetts: Paraclete Press, 2014)

[9] Ibid., 1.

[10] Ignatian Style. When I say, "putting myself into the scripture Ignatian style," what I'm describing is basically prayer with imagination. David Fleming, S.J. explained it well in his book, *What is Ignatian Spirituality?* (Chicago, IL: Loyola Press, 2008) He said we can imagine placing ourselves fully within a gospel story. We become a character in the scripture and then notice all that is going on around us–using our senses. We smell, we hear, we see as if we are there. We notice how the people are responding to one another or to Jesus. Through our imagination, Jesus, as well as others, are experienced as living.

[11] Flynn, *The 7 Secrets of Confession,* 49.

[12] Ibid., 49

[13] Hahn, *Lord Have Mercy,* 66.

[14] Fr. Andrew Apostoli, *Fatima Today* (San Francisco: Ignatius Press, 2010), 239.

[15] Hahn, *Lord Have Mercy,* 151.

[16] *Address of His Holiness Benedict XVI to the Confessors Who Serve in the Four Papal Basilicas of Rome,* February 19, 2007.

[17] Jason Evert, *Saint John Paul the Great. His Five Loves* (Lakewood Colorado: Totus Tuus Press, 2014), 189.

[18] Kowalska, *Diary of St. Maria Faustina Kowalska,* Notebook VI, paragraph 1602.

[19] Hahn, *Lord Have Mercy,* 147.

Chapter 6

[1] *14 Rules of Discernment.* The fourteen rules of discernment, systematized by St. Ignatius of Loyola, are guidelines based on insights and responses from his spiritual life and personal experiences. Of the fourteen rules of spiritual discernment, outlined in Fr. Tim Gallagher's book, *The Discernment of Spirits: An Ignatian Guide for Everyday Living* (New York: Crossword Publishing Company, 2005), desolation is rule no. 4. Basically, it is considered a time of trial in one's faith walk. Fr. Tim Gallagher writes that in all discernment of spirits, desolation is most valuable and encouraging. Ignatius of Loyola defines spiritual desolation in this way: "The fourth is of spiritual desolate. I call desolation the contrary of the third rule, (consolation) such as darkness of soul, disturbance in it, movement flow and early things, disquiet from various agitations and temptations, moving to lack of confidence, without hope, without love, finding oneself totally slothful, tepic, sad, and as if separated from one's Creator and Lord. For just as consolation is contrary to desolation, in the same way the thoughts that come from consolation are contrary to the thoughts that come from desolation" (60).

[2] Venial sins. The Catechism of the Catholic Church explains that there are two types of sin: mortal and venial sins. There are

also different classes of sin. They can be differentiated by the commandments they violate, and whether the nature of the sin concerns God, neighbor or oneself. They are also divided into spiritual and carnal sins or as sins in thought, word, and deed, or omission (CCC, 1853). Specifically, sins are evaluated as to their gravity in either category of moral or venial commission. Briefly, mortal sin is more detrimental as it "destroys charity in the heart of man by a grave violation of God's law," and turns one away from God to a lesser good than him. In venial sin, there is continued charity; but the sin can offend and wound (CCC, 1856). For a more comprehensive understanding, you might want to read, in its entirety (CCC, 1856-1864).

[3] Fr. Thomas Dubay, *Prayer Primer: Igniting a Fire Within* (San Francisco, CA: Ignatius Press, 2002), 65.

[4] Fr. Thomas Dubay, *Fire Within: St. Teresa of Avila, St. John of the Cross and the Gospel-On Prayer* (San Francisco, CA: Ignatius Press, 1989), 68.

[5] Ralph Martin, *Fulfillment of all Desire: A Guidebook for the Journey to God Based on the Wisdom of the Saints* (Steubenville, OH: Emmaus Road Publishing, 2006), 131.

[6] See ENDNOTE 6 from Chapter 2, explaining Carmelite Spirituality and a "Rule of Life."

[7] Sr. Mary Alphonsetta Haneman, *The Spiritualty of St. Teresa of Avila* (Boston, MA: Pauline Books & Media, 1983), 19.

[8] Haneman, *The Spiritualty of St. Teresa of Avila*, 19.

[9] Martin, *Fulfillment of all Desire*, 122.

[10] Fr. Thomas Dubay, *Prayer Primer: Igniting a Fire Within* (San Francisco: Ignatius Press), 55.

[11] Dubay, *Fire Within*, 82.

[12] Jean-Baptiste Chautard, O.C.D.S. *Soul of the Apostolate* (Charlotte, NC: TAN Books, 1974), 85.

[13] Ibid.

[14] Ibid.

[15] Martin, *Fulfillment of all Desire,* 96.

[16] Dubay, *Fire Within,* 52.

[17] Martin, *Fulfillment of all Desire,* 132.

[18] Pope St. John Paul II Apostolic Letter, *Novo Millennio Ineuente* (6 January 2001), para. 39.

[19] Tim Gray, *Praying Scripture for Change: An Introduction to Lectio Divina* (Westchester, PA: Ascension Press, 2009), 4.

[20] Ibid., 68.

[21] Pope Benedict XVI, *Address of His Holiness on the 40th Anniversary of the Dogmatic Constitution on Divine Revelation "Dei Verbum,"* September 16, 2005, Castel Gandolfo.

Chapter 7

[1] Ralph Martin, *Fulfillment of all Desire* (Steubenville, OH: Emmaus Road Publishing, 2006).

[2] Thomas Dubay, *Fire Within: St. Teresa of Avila, St. John of the Cross and the Gospel* (San Francisco: Ignatius Press, 1989).

[3] Thomas Dubay, *Fire Within: St. Teresa of Avila, St. John of the Cross and the Gospel-On Prayer* (San Francisco, CA: Ignatius Press, 1989), 57.

[4] Thomas Dubay, *Prayer Primer: Igniting a Fire Within* (San Francisco, CA: Ignatius Press, 2002), 66.

[5] *Ignatius Catholic Study Bible* New Testament, Second Edition RSV (San Francisco: Ignatius Press, 2010), 129.

6 Fr. Robert Spitzer, S.J., *Five Pillars of the Spiritual Life: A Practical Guide to Prayer for the Active People* (San Francisco, CA: Ignatius Press, 2008), 100.

7 Spitzer, *Five Pillars of the Spiritual Life,* 101.

8 Ibid., 101.

9 Fr. Eugene McCaffrey, *Let Nothing Trouble You: Teresa The Woman, The Guide, and the Storyteller* (Blackrock, Co. Dublin: Columba Press, 2015), 96-98.

10 Dubay, *Fire Within,* 34.

11 Ibid., 35.

12 Ibid., 15.

13 St. Teresa of Avila (translated by Kieran Kavanaugh, O.C.D. and Otilio Rodriguez, O.C.D., prepared by Kieran Kavanaugh, O.C.D. and Carol Lisi, O.C.D.S.) *The Interior Castle Study Edition* (Washington, DC: ICS Publications, Institute of Carmelite Studies, 2010), 33.

14 Dubay, *Fire Within,* 117.

15 Dan Burke and Anthony Liles, *30 Days with Teresa of Avila,* Navigating the Interior Life Series (Steubenville, OH: Emmaus Road Publishing, 2015), 33.

16 Ibid., 34.

17 Dubay, *Fire Within,* 58.

18 Ralph Martin, *The Fulfillment of All Desire,* Annotated Edition (Steubenville, OH: Emmaus Road Publishing, 2006), 286.

19 Ibid., 290.

20 Dubay, *Fire Within,* 85.

21 Martin, *The Fulfillment of All Desire,* 291.

22 Ibid., 291.

[23] St. Teresa of Avila (Prepared by Kieran Kavanaugh), *The Way of Perfection: A Study Edition*, (Washington, DC: ICS Publications, Institute of Carmelite Studies), 270.

[24] Martin, *The Fulfillment of All Desire*, 296.

[25] St. Teresa of Avila, *The Way of Perfection*, 170-171.

[26] Fr. Marc Foley, O.C.D., *The Dark Night: Psychological Experience and Spiritual Reality* (Washington, DC: ICS Publications, Institute of Carmelite Studies, 2018), 80.

[27] Ibid., 80.

[28] Ibid., 153.

[29] Mother Teresa with Brian Kolodiejchuk, M.C., editor, *Mother Teresa: Come Be My Light: The Private Writings of the Saint of Calcutta* (New York, NY: Doubleday Religion, 2007) Preface.

[30] David Scott, *The Love That Made Mother Teresa*. From 2005, article: https://oldarchive.godspy.com/reviews/Finding-Joy-in-the-Darkest-Night-The-Divine-Abandonment-of-Mother-Teresa-by-David-Scott.cfm.htm.

Chapter 8

[1] Fr. Michael E. Gaitley, *33 Days to Morning Glory: A Do-It-Yourself Retreat In Preparation for Marian Consecration* (Stockbridge, MA: Marian Press, 2018), 25.

[2] Janice T. Connell, *Meetings with Mary: Visions of the Blessed Mother* (New York, NY: Ballantine Books, 1995), 52.

[3] Ibid., 52.

[4] Ibid., 54.

---

[5] Jason Evert, *Saint John Paul the Great: His Five Loves* (San Francisco: Ignatius Press, 2014), 165.

[6] Archbishop Fulton J. Sheen in *The Cries of Jesus from the Cross: An Anthology* (Nashua, NH: Sophia Institute Press, 2018), 112.

[7] Fr. Michael E. Gaitley, *33 Days to Morning Glory: A Do-It-Yourself Retreat in Preparation for Marian Consecration* (Stockbridge, MA: Marian Press, 2018), 90.

[8] Ibid., 98.

[9] Reference Chapter 4 Endnote 1: Infused contemplation.

[10] Gaitley, *33 Days to Morning Glory*, 26.

[11] Mirjana Soldo, *My Heart Will Triumph* (Cocoa, FL: CatholicShop Publishing, 2016), 27.

[12] Janice T. Connell, *Meetings with Mary: Visions of the Blessed Mother* (New York, NY: Ballantine Books, 1995), xviii.

[13] See ENDNOTE 4 from Chapter 1: Laying on of hands.

[14] https://missionandshrine.org/

[15] Scott Hahn, *Signs of Life: 40 Catholic Customs and Their Biblical Roots* (New York, NY: Doubleday Religion, 2009), 230.

[16] Ibid., 232.

[17] Jeff Cavins and Thomas Smith, *Revelation: The Kingdom Yet to Come* video (AscensionPress.com)

[18] "The Memorare." Remember, O most gracious Virgin Mary, that never was it known that anyone who fled to thy protection, implored thy help, or sought thy intercession was left unaided. Inspired with this confidence, I fly to thee, O Virgin of virgins, my Mother; to thee do I come; before thee I stand, sinful and sorrowful. O Mother of the Word Incarnate, despise not my petitions, but in thy mercy hear and answer me. Amen."

[19] In the Catholic Church, there are three classes of sacred relics. The first-class is a part of the saint's body. The second-class is a piece of the saint's clothing or something used by the saint while the third-class is an object which has been touched to a first-class relic. In the Council of Trent, 16th century, it was decided that the veneration of the saints and the relics and the holy bodies of the holy martyrs and of the others who dwell with Christ are to be honored by the faithful. https://www.catholiceducation.org/en/culture/catholic-contributions/church-teaching-on-relics.html

[20] Fr. Timothy M. Gallagher, O.M.V., *The Discernment of Spirits: An Ignatian Guide for Everyday Living* (New York, NY: The Crossroad Publishing Company, 2005), 74.

[21] Edward Sri, *Praying the Rosary Like Never Before: Encounter the Wonder of Heaven and Earth* (Cincinnati, OH: Servant Books/Franciscan Media), 24.

[22] Mirjana Soldo, *My Heart Will Triumph* (Cocoa, FL: CatholicShop Publishing: 2016), 117.

[23] Ibid., 33.

[24] Evert, *Saint John Paul the Great*, 167.

[25] Soldo, *My Heart Will Triumph*, 15.

[26] Ibid., 97.

Chapter 9

[1] Fr. Michael E. Gaitley, *33 Days to Morning Glory: A Do-It-Yourself Retreat in Preparation for Marian Consecration* (Stockbridge, MA: Marian Press, 2018), 68.

[2] Ibid., 73.

[3] St. Louis de Montfort, *The Secret of Mary* (Rockford, IL: TAN Books & Publishers, Inc., 1998), 13.

[4] Fr. Andrew Apostoli, *Fatima For Today* (San Francisco, CA: Ignatius Press, 2010), X.

[5] Ibid., 23.

[6] Ibid., 27.

[7] Ibid., 35.

[8] Ibid., 79.

[9] Ibid., 66.

[10] Gaitley, *33 Days to Morning Glory*, 101.

[11] Ibid., 25.

[12] Ibid., 20.

[13] Fr. Hugh Gillespie, *Total Consecration to Mary* (Bayshore, NY: Montfort Publications, 2011), 128.

[14] Ibid., 129.

[15] Fr. Slavko Barbaric, O.F.M., *Pray with the Heart! Medjugorje Manual of Prayer* (Steubenville, OH: Franciscan University Press, 1988), 9.

[16] St. John of the Cross is the authority on detachments. Another good book: *Drinking from a Dry Well* by Thomas Greene

[17] WEBSITE: https://www.medjugorjemiracles.com/2014/01/medjugorje-message-of-january-2-2014/

[18] Thomas Dubay, *Fire Within: St. Teresa of Avila, St. John of the Cross and the Gospel-On Prayer* (San Francisco, CA: Ignatius Press, 1989), 134.

[19] Luiz Sergio Solimeo, *Fatima: A Message More Urgent Than Ever* (Spring Grove, PA: The American Society for the Defense of Tradition, Family and Property – TFP, 2016), 42.

[20] Ibid., 43.

²¹ Gaitley, *33 Days to Morning Glory*, 75.

²² Ibid., 76.

²³ Ibid., 76.

²⁴ Mirjana Soldo, *My Heart Will Triumph* (Cocoa, FL: CatholicShop Publishing, 2016), 33.

²⁵ Ibid., 369.

²⁶ Gaitley, *33 Days to Morning Glory*, 63.

Chapter 10

¹ Fr. John Hardon, S.J. (Retreat for Handmaids of the Precious Blood) notes

² Fr. Michael Gaitley, *The Second Greatest Story Ever Told: Now is the Time of Mercy* (Stockbridge, MA: Marian Father of the Immaculate Conception, 2015), 175.

³ Gaitley, *The Second Greatest Story Ever Told*, 72.

⁴ Ibid., 55.

⁵ St. Maria Faustina Kowalska, *Diary of St. Maria Faustina Kowalska: Divine Mercy in My Soul* (Stockbridge, MA: Marian Press, 2012) *Notebook* II, paragraph 949.

⁶ https://www.thedivinemercy.org/articles/gods-love-flower-mercy-fruit, *part five of the series "God's Love is the Flower - Mercy the Fruit." September 12, 2019.*

⁷Fr. John Hampsch, CMF, *The Awesome Mercy of God* (Cincinnati, OH: Franciscan Media, 2006), https://shop.franciscanmedia.org/products/the-awesome-mercy-of-god.

⁸ Fr. Michael E. Gaitley, MIC, *Consoling the Heart of Jesus: A Do-It-Yourself Retreat.* (Stockbridge, MA: Marian Press, 2011).

⁹ Gaitley, *The Second Greatest Story Ever Told*, 28.

[10] Mary Fabyan Windeatt, *Saint Margaret Mary and the Promises of the Sacred Heart of Jesus* (Charlotte, NC: Tan Publications, 2012), 94-115.

[11] Fr. Andrew Apostoli, *Fatima For Today* (San Francisco, CA: Ignatius Press, 2010), 28.

[12] See Chapter 2 Endnote 16, Angel of Peace Fatima Prayers.

[13] Apostoli, *Fatima For Today*, 27.

[14] Gaitley, *Consoling the Heart of Jesus*, 49.

[15] Ibid., 50.

[16] Apostoli, *Fatima For Today*, 78 – 79.

[17] Ibid., 148-149.

[18] Gaitley, *The Second Greatest Story Ever Told*, 130.

[19] Kowalska, *Diary of St. Maria Faustina Kowalska.*

[20] Ibid., paragraph 742.

[21] Fr. Michael E. Gaitley, *33 Days to Morning Glory: A Do-It-Yourself Retreat In Preparation for Marian Consecration* (Stockbridge, MA: Marian Press, 2018), 103.

[22] Kowalska, *Diary of St. Maria Faustina Kowalska*, paragraphs 1605, 1567, and 35.

[23] Gaitley, *The Second Greatest Story Ever Told*, 72.

[24] Ibid., 74.

[25] Kowalska, *Diary of St. Maria Faustina Kowalska*, paragraph 476.

[26] Ibid., paragraph 84.

[27] https://www.thedivinemercy.org/message/devotions.

[28] Kowalska, *Diary of St. Maria Faustina Kowalska*, paragraph 49.

[29] Ibid., paragraph 699.

[30] Ibid., paragraph 300.

[31] Gaitley, *The Second Greatest Story Ever Told*, 70.

[32]Vatican website, accessed April 17, 2021 - http://www.vatican.va/content/john-paul-ii/en/homilies/2002/documents/hf_jp-ii_hom_20020817_shrine-divine-mercy.html

Afterword

[1] Fr. Jacques Phillipe, *Thirsting for Prayer* (New York: Scepter Publishing, 2014), v.

[2] Fr. Michael Gaitley, *The Second Greatest Story Ever Told: Now is the Time of Mercy* (Stockbridge, MA: Marian Father of the Immaculate Conception, 2015), 113.

[3] Website, accessed June 26, 2021 - https://www.catholicnewsagency.com/news/44296/us-and-canada-to-be-consecrated-to-mary-mother-of-the-church.

[4] Janice T. Connell, in *Meetings with Mary: Visions of the Blessed Mother* (New York, NY: Ballantine Books, 1995), 8.

[5] Gaitley, *The Second Greatest Story Ever Told*, 174.

[6] Fr. Chris Alar, *Explaining the Faith Series: Understanding Divine Mercy* (Stockbridge, Mass: Marian Press, 2021).

[7] Gaitley, *The Second Greatest Story Ever Told*, 97.

[8] Ibid., 107.

[9] Ibid., 106.

[10] Ibid., 106.

[11] St. Maria Faustina Kowalska, *Diary of St. Maria Faustina Kowalska: Divine Mercy in My Soul* (Stockbridge, MA: Marian Press, 2012), paragraph 1732.

Made in the USA
Monee, IL
26 September 2022

14396842R00164